THE MILITARY POWER
OF THE PRESIDENT

MICHAEL KRONENWETTER

THE
MILITARY
POWER
OF THE PRESIDENT

1988
FRANKLIN WATTS
NEW YORK LONDON TORONTO SYDNEY

Photographs courtesy of: The Bettmann Archive: pp. 13, 25, 32, 40, 42, 44, 47, 49, 52, 55 (bottom), 58 (Pach), 64; UPI/Bettmann Newsphotos: pp. 21, 85, 87, 92, 100 (top), 109, 113 (Reuters), 120, 126 (top, Reuters; bottom, UPI), 127 (top, Reuters; bottom, UPI); Mansell Collection: p. 55 (top); Pictorial Parade: p. 60; Valentine Museum, Richmond, Virginia: p. 68 (Cook Collection); Frederic Remington Art Museum: p. 78; ROTHCO Cartoons: pp. 82 (Kirk), 100 (bottom, Garland), 111 (Dennis Renault), 116 (Josh Beutel).

Library of Congress Cataloging-in-Publication Data

Kronenwetter, Michael.
The military power of the president/Michael Kronenwetter.
p. cm.
Bibliography: p.
Includes index.
Summary: Examines the extent of military power held by America's commander-in-chief—a subject of much debate since the founding of the nation.
ISBN 0-531-10590-3
1. Executive power—United States—Juvenile literature.
2. Presidents—United States—Juvenile literature. 3. War and emergency powers—United States—Juvenile literature.
[1. Executive power. 2. Presidents. 3. War and emergency powers.]
I. Title.
JK558.K76 1988
353.03′22—dc19   88-17013 CIP AC

CONTENTS

086992

THE MILITARY POWER
OF THE PRESIDENT

INTRODUCTION
GRENADA
OCTOBER 1983

The attack came suddenly and by surprise. It was Tuesday morning, October 25, 1983. It was so early that the sky was still dark, and most of the people on the little Caribbean island of Grenada were still asleep. Suddenly, many of them were awakened by the roar of American jet fighters streaking overhead. Those who stumbled outside near the island's southwest corner must have been astonished to see hundreds of strange black shapes hovering in the air above them. As they watched, the mysterious shapes formed themselves into men and parachutes. They were U.S. Army Rangers floating down from the sky.

On the eastern end of the island, other Grenadians were roused by the whirring of American helicopter gunships swooping down onto the runways of Pearls Airport. The island's only working airport, Pearls was usually used only for ordinary commercial traffic— mostly, in fact, to carry vacationing American tourists in and out of the little nation. But the more than 1,900 Americans who arrived in Grenada that day were not there for a vacation. They had come as part of an invading force.

— 9 —

There had been no declaration of war against Grenada. The U.S. forces had not been sent by Congress, but by President Ronald Reagan. He was responding, he later explained, to a request from several of Grenada's Caribbean neighbors. (The American troops were joined in the invasion by token forces from some of those nations.) Grenada had recently been torn by conflict among its Marxist leadership. The popular prime minister, Maurice Bishop, had been killed. The neighbors were worried that the troubles on the island might spread. What's more, they were concerned by reports that Cubans were on the island to build a military airfield that could be used as a communist military base in the Caribbean.

Most Grenadians seemed to welcome the invasion, and many Americans applauded it. Most of the rest of the world, however, condemned it. The majority of the United Nations Security Council voted for a resolution denouncing it as a "flagrant violation of international law." Not one member of the Security Council supported the United States in the vote. (France voted for the resolution, and Great Britain abstained.) The U.S. itself eventually vetoed the resolution.

Regardless of what other nations thought of it, the invasion was successful. Within days, Grenada was under American control. Within two weeks all resistance had been put down.

According to the U.S. Constitution, it is up to Congress to declare when the United States is to go to war. Yet President Reagan had ordered the military invasion of Grenada on his own. True, he had informed some congressional leaders of what would happen, but only after he had already ordered the invasion to begin.[1] How could the president do it? How could he justify acting without a congressional declaration of war?

One way was by historical precedent. In the two hundred years that the United States has been a country, American armed forces have been involved in over two hundred separate hostilities away from American soil—either in foreign nations or on the high seas.[2] (And that doesn't even include internal military conflicts like the Revolutionary War, the Indian Wars, or the War Between the States.) At least eleven of these hostilities have involved large-scale military engagements over extended periods of time. Some involved tens of thousands, even hundreds of thousands, of casualties. Several are commonly referred to as "wars" in the history books. Most, if not all, involved actions legally defined as "acts of war."

But in spite of all that, Congress has actually declared war only five times in our entire history.[3] All the other times, the military acted primarily on the authority of the president in office at the time, not of Congress.

Although President Reagan was acting like many of his predecessors, debate still rages over whether he was justified in the actions he took in ordering the invasion of Grenada, and, more recently, in involving the United States more deeply in the Persian Gulf conflagration—without the approval of Congress.

It is not a new debate. It has been fought out between presidents and Congresses for two centuries. In order to explore this debate, we need to better understand the nature and mechanics of war itself.

THE NATURE OF WAR

War is a general term used to describe certain kinds of armed conflicts. Wars can be large or small. Some of them are fought between two nations. Others involve large numbers of countries fighting either individually, each against the others, or in alliances.

Although the term "war" is usually reserved for conflicts involving at least one national government, not all wars are fought *between* nations. Wars can also be fought between factions, or groups, within a single country.

A revolutionary war, for example, is fought between the government of a country and a group of citizens attempting to overthrow that government by force. Our own Civil War was an example of still another kind of internal war, in which two groups of state governments fought with each other over whether or not they should remain one country.

THE DANGERS OF WAR

William Tecumseh Sherman was a Union general in that Civil War. Speaking to a group of war veterans years later, he gave one of the most grim—and most famous—of all definitions of war. "There is many a boy here today who looks on war as all glory," he told them. "But, boys, it is all hell."[1]

Sherman was in a position to know. He has been described as the prophet of modern total war. That description may be overstated, since he never ordered the kind of ruthless killing of civilians that has become a commonplace in some twentieth-century wars, but in his infamous "march to the sea," he and his army of 68,000 men laid waste to a large area of Georgia. They burned and slashed their way three hundred miles across the state, devastating the countryside. Instead of engaging the military forces of the Confederacy, they concentrated on destroying the economy of Georgia and its ability to support those military forces: in partic-

The Battle of Atlanta launched Sherman's infamous "march to the sea."

ular, they targeted the state's crops and food supplies. One purpose of Sherman's advance was to intimidate and demoralize the population: to make the experience of war so terrible for them that their will to fight would be destroyed, along with their property.[2]

If Sherman's description of war as "all hell" was true in the nineteenth century, it is even more true in the twentieth. The destructive power of Sherman's entire army was not equal to the power in the warheads attached to a single nuclear missile. There is no power more awesome—or more dangerous—than the power to wage war. In wartime, the ordinary rules of human (and national) conduct are suspended. The most fundamental civil rights are often disregarded. Acts that at any other time would be considered terrible crimes, up to and including what would otherwise be considered mass murder, become "acceptable." What is more, the power to wage war includes the power to put the safety of the nation, and of every person in it, in danger. A country at war is a country at risk. In modern times, it may be a country in danger of total destruction.

The power to wage war implies not only the authority to defend one's own nation, but to attack other nations as well: whether by armed invasion, or at long range by the use of bombs and missiles. Ultimately, it includes not just the power to destroy the peace of a single nation, or even of a group of nations, but the peace of the entire world. Despite this fact, countries are left on their own to their decisions about if and when to go to war.

Sometimes, countries are eager to go to war—sure of the righteousness of their cause, confident of an easy victory. At other times, they are reluctant; they see no other option, but are fearful that they might be destroyed. At still other times, they go to war divided, some citizens sure of the rightness of the action, others bitterly opposed to it. Still, nations keep deciding to fight. It's been said that there hasn't been a day in the twentieth century—if ever—when the entire world has been at peace. Why? What could possibly be worth the destruction brought about by war?

REASONS FOR WAR

Some people, called *pacifists*, believe that nothing can be worth going to war. They argue that warfare, particularly modern warfare, is so terrible that nothing could possibly justify its risks.[3] Pacifists, however, seem to be in the minority in most nations. Certainly, few, if any, governments are seriously committed to pacifism. Although most governments give lip service to their devotion to peace, most also maintain military forces—and use them.

Some scholars believe that war is not so much a matter of government policy as of instinct. They believe that human beings are naturally aggressive, and combative. Whatever people or their governments may *think* they are fighting about, what they are really doing is giving vent to an elemental human inclination to violence.

In this respect, scientists of societal behavior—called ethologists—argue that people are much like many animals who, when they meet other animals in the wild, immediately bare their fangs and start to fight with each other. They say that nations—which are, after all, made up of human beings, and governed by them—are basically no different from individuals. They share the same instinct to fight with, and ultimately to dominate, each other.[4]

Other scientists argue that this is nonsense. There are many species of animals that show no basic instinct to do battle, just as there are many individual human beings who exhibit no violent behavior. They say the analogy (or comparison) between animals, humans, and nation states is false. Human beings are not brute animals, and nations are not individual human beings. What may be true of one of these things is not necessarily true of the others.

Still other scholars are convinced that the true causes of war are more economic and social than psychological. For them the underlying cause of war is the gulf between the rich and the poor. There are many different versions of these economic theories of the roots of war, most of which rely to some extent on the theories of Karl Marx.[5] Most of them are based on the assumption that rich and powerful nations will inevitably try to profit from and exploit poor nations. This leads to two different kinds of war. The first is war between the rich and the poor, in which the rich try to impose their will and the poor resist. The second is war between two or more rich and powerful nations over which of them shall be allowed to exploit the poor ones.

There are many other theories of war. The famous nineteenth-century Prussian military strategist Karl von Clausewitz, for example, believed that war was merely a tactic for governments to use to accomplish whatever goals they might want to achieve. He described war simply as a continuation of diplomacy by other means.[6]

All countries have things they want to do, and things they want other countries to do. Or not to do. They might want trade with a given country, for example, or the diplomatic support from that country, or guarantees of military security, or any of a number of other things. War, and the threat of war, are a means by which governments can pressure other governments into doing what they want them to do. When negotiation and other political and economic pressures fail, force—in the form of military power—can be applied.

Most modern governments seem to regard war more or less the way von Clausewitz did. They believe that decisions about war should be made rationally, and only after weighing the possible dangers and benefits. In reality, a variety of motives seem to play a part in any nation's decisions about war and peace. Some of these are, in fact, national and diplomatic. Others are not rational at all. Among the most common are:

SELF-DEFENSE. Most governments consider it their first and most important duty to defend their country against its enemies. Very often, then, countries go to war because they feel they are threatened from the outside.

Sometimes these threats are direct and obvious: the Japanese attack on Pearl Harbor in 1941, for example, was a clear threat to the defenses of the western United States, and the United States immediately declared war on Japan. Sometimes the threat is less clear. Countries have been known to go to war because of the *fear* that another country was planning to attack. Some have even attacked other countries themselves, in order to prevent potential enemies from becoming powerful enough to consider attacking them.

NATIONALISM. In the modern world, countries tend to be jealous of their national identity. They believe that they have a right to national independence. They resent any effort by other nations to interfere in their affairs. Many wars have been caused by the desire of one nation to assert its independence from another. This is true, for example, of the American Revolution, and of the many wars of independence fought by Third World countries against the more powerful European countries that had colonized them. Since the colonial powers usually controlled the formal governments of those countries, these wars have tended to be revolutionary, like the Mau Mau revolt in Kenya of the 1950s, which led to the country's independence from the British.

Another aspect of nationalism is simple national pride. People sometimes feel that their country has been slighted, or insulted in some way. Sometimes this feeling results in an impulse to strike out militarily, to "avenge" the nation's honor, or to soothe the public's injured pride. This impulse may explain at least some of the overwhelming support that actions such as the invasion of Grenada in 1983 and the bombing of Libya in 1986 received from the American public.

American hostages had been taken by Iranian students backed by that country's government, and held for more than a year. What's more, Americans had been subjected for years to what seemed like an unending series of terrorist acts around the world. And the United States—which prided itself on being the most powerful country in the world—seemed unable to do anything about any of it. Many Americans were tired of being "pushed around" by "little" countries. They saw the invasions of Grenada and Libya as ways of reasserting American pride and power in the world.

IDEOLOGY. Many conflicts are fueled by differences in political and social beliefs. Many wars are fought not so much between two social or economic classes as between people with two different points of view about how a country—or the world—should be run.

There were several reasons for the American Revolution of 1776. Some of them were nationalistic, others economic, but there was also a strong ideological basis for the revolution. Thomas Jefferson and other revolutionaries based their right to rebel against British rule on what amounted to a liberal political ideology: belief in the personal and political liberty of the individual. Other colonists opposed the Revolution on equally ideological grounds: the belief that the power and authority of the state, represented by the king, had to be honored and obeyed, whatever the cost to the individual.

World Wars I and II were examples of another kind of ideological conflict. Nations (such as Germany and Japan) that believed in rule by authoritarian, autocratic governments fought nations with democratic governments, such as the United States, France, and Britain. Many people on the Allied side believed they were fighting not just for their own countries but for the principle of democracy itself.

Today, the struggle between capitalism and communism underlies many conflicts in the world. Western nations regard communism as an evil ideology which justifies the political, material, and spiritual repression of people. Communists, on the other hand, regard capitalism as an evil ideology which justifies the exploitation and impoverishment of people. Each side accuses the other of wanting to impose its own ideology on the world by force. The communist government of Cuba, for example, has supplied assistance to a number of communist guerrilla movements around the world. American politicians, on the other hand, often justify military actions—including the war in Vietnam—on the grounds that they are necessary to stop the advancement of communism.

RELIGION. Differences in religious belief have long provided one of the main justifications for wars. Ironically, in fact, religious wars have always been among the bloodiest and most merciless wars.

From 1095 to 1271 A.D., the Christians of Europe launched no less than nine separate military crusades to "win back" the holy lands of the Bible from the Muslims who lived there. The Muslims, in turn, have periodically launched *jihads* (holy wars) of their own against those they refer to as "unbelievers."

The religious tensions left in the wake of the Protestant Reformation of the sixteenth century helped to fuel a variety of wars throughout Europe. These included, among other conflicts, the so-called Peasants' War, the

Thirty Years War, and the English Civil War. The desire to bring the Christian God to the "heathens" of Asia, Africa, and the Americas helped to justify many bloody wars of colonization in the past few centuries. Even in this century, wars in many parts of the world, from Ireland to the Middle East, have been fought at least partly along religious lines. At this writing, Sunni and Shiite Muslims have been fighting each other for six years in a terribly destructive war between Iraq and Iran.

RACISM. Hostility between races has played an important part in starting a large number of wars. Even more importantly, it has helped to increase the intensity and viciousness of wars started for other reasons. When a wartime enemy is of another race, propagandists tend to incite the racial prejudice of the people to stir them into greater efforts against the enemy. The Nazi government of Germany came to power on a tide of anti-Semitism (hatred and fear of Jewish people) and proclaimed that it was fighting against "mongrel races" during World War II. Even in the United States, racial prejudice was appealed to during that same war by talk of the "yellow peril"—the Japanese.

MILITARISM. In some societies, governmental and military authority is held by the same people: the leaders of the country's armed forces. As professional soldiers, they tend to be proud of their military skills and to look for opportunities to exercise them. They look, too, for disputes that can help them justify their rule. For instance, the military class in Germany helped bring that nation to war in 1914. In such societies, war isn't regarded as a grim necessity, undertaken only in extreme circumstances. Instead, it is thought of as a positive condition. The desire to take part in military conflict becomes a motive for war in itself.

A more subtle form of militarism can be seen in the tendency of nations such as the United States and the

President Dwight D. Eisenhower (in front jeep wearing a suit) *reviews troops in Korea. Like George Washington, William Henry Harrison, Andrew Jackson, Benjamin Harrison, Ulysses S. Grant, and Zachary Taylor, Eisenhower was a general before he became president.*

Soviet Union to build huge amounts of expensive weapons. When so many weapons are built and so much of a nation's economy becomes dependent on building them, there may be a kind of unconscious pressure to use them—if only to justify all that effort.

MISUNDERSTANDING. Still another reason for war is simple misunderstanding—the miscalculations of governments. There is a good deal of evidence, for example, that one of the major causes of World War I was misunderstanding between the leaders of the nations of Europe. This was particularly ironic considering that many of those leaders were related to each other.[7]

Few wars can be completely explained by any one of the motives mentioned above. Most wars have probably been brought about by a combination of these and other factors.

MAKING DECISIONS

Every society has its own way of deciding if (or when) to go to war, and how to conduct the war once it has started. In the United States, these decisions are shared between the legislative and the executive branches of the federal government: between Congress and the president.

This division of the war-making power has been an uneasy, constantly shifting arrangement. It has been a cause of enormous tension between the two branches of government ever since it was first established by the Constitution of the United States in 1787. It continues to be a source of tension and controversy today.

In very general terms, the extent of the presidential war power is decided by four factors: the Constitution of the United States, traditional practices, public opinion—and the relative strength and determination of the president and Congress at any given time.

In the next chapter, we will examine what the Constitution says about the war powers. In later chapters, we will examine how its words have been put into practice.

WHAT THE CONSTITUTION SAYS

The American Revolution was a joint enterprise of thirteen rebellious colonies. However, even though they thought of themselves as independent states, they still felt the need for a federal (or central) government, if only to oversee the conduct of the war.

At first, they improvised their government as they went along. Eventually, however, a formal structure was established with the adoption of the Articles of Confederation, which were written in 1777 and went into effect in 1781. That first government was relatively weak, as befitted a loose alliance of states, but it served the new nation through the rest of the Revolutionary War, and even for a few years beyond.

In time, however, it became clear to many people that the government needed strengthening. The young country was plagued by serious problems that the government seemed unable to do anything about. One of the most basic problems was the fact that the division of authority between the state and federal governments was unclear. The individual states tended to go their own ways, often working at cross purposes to the federal government. Some states were signing treaties with each other and even with the Indians, bypassing the federal government altogether. Another major problem was the national debt, left over from the Revolution. The federal government was having trouble getting the states to pay their share of that debt. Even when states were willing to pay, there was the question of what kind of money they should use. Some states issued currency that they promised to exchange for gold and silver, and their money was prized by everyone. But some of the states issued paper money that couldn't be exchanged for anything at all, and their money was considered almost worthless by many creditors. Was it reasonable to expect one state to pay its share of the national debt in gold, while another paid its share in paper?

SHAYS' REBELLION

Among their other differences, the states had very different taxation policies. Some made things easy on their citizens. They either imposed low taxes or inflated their currencies (each state had its own) with so much paper money that what taxes they had were easy to pay. Other states, particularly those in New England, took an opposite approach. They imposed such heavy taxes that many of their citizens, especially the farmers, were being financially destroyed.

Not surprisingly, there was a great deal of anger among the farmers in those states, particularly when they saw the easy tax policies of other states. In Massachusetts, that anger caused what looked to some people like a second American revolution. Daniel Shays, a farmer and ex-captain of the Continental Army, put together a rag-tag force of armed men to resist the states' high-taxation policies. Massachusetts borrowed money from some wealthy businessmen and

*A brawl during Shays' Rebellion,
the 1780s uprising against land taxes*

organized a militia to fight Shays' little army. The bloody
culmination of what came to be called Shays' Rebellion
came in a battle in a snowstorm near Springfield, Massachusetts, in January of 1787, when the militia put
Shays and his men to rout.[1]

Shays' farmers were a small, militarily ineffective
bunch. They probably never really had a chance to
stand up against an organized, well-financed state militia. They might, however, have managed to stand up
against the federal government—at least for a while.

That government was militarily ineffective: under the Articles of Confederation, it could have no standing peacetime army. If it had needed one to put down a more effective rebellion, or for any other reason, it would have had to spend a lot of time just trying to organize one before it could act. The way things were going, it couldn't count on the states to supply it with soldiers anyway.

MAKING A CONSTITUTION

The new nation held a Federal Convention just a few months after the defeat of Shays' Rebellion. Its stated purpose was simply to amend the Articles of Confederation. As it turned out, however, it did much more than that. It scrapped the Articles altogether, and completely redesigned the American government.

To replace the Articles as a blueprint for that government, the Convention drew up a new document: the Constitution of the United States of America. The Articles had guided the new country for less than a decade; the Constitution would serve it for the next two centuries and beyond. It would be the fundamental law of the nation. Everything done by that government— including declaring and waging war—would have to be done in accordance with it.

THE NEED FOR A
FEDERAL WAR POWER

The fifty-five delegates who gathered in Philadelphia in the spring of 1787 had many things on their minds. Not the least of their concerns was the recent bloody rebellion in Massachusetts. As the Convention began, that state still had its militia under arms. Among the major issues to be discussed were the questions of war and peace, and how the new government they were about to establish would deal with those questions.

The first question that had to be answered was: Did the new federal government really need any war powers at all?

There was little, if any, disagreement among the delegates that the new country would need to defend itself if it were attacked.[2] However, as Massachusetts had already demonstrated, the individual states were capable of raising their own militias. Representatives of some states thought that such militias would be enough. They were jealous of their states' authority and worried that the new federal government might try to exert too much power. They feared that a federal army might be used to coerce the states, and to override their authority by force. This did in fact happen when the southern states tried to secede at the time of the Civil War.

Weighted against this fear were several strong arguments in favor of a federal war power. War with a foreign power was a constant threat. After all, three potential enemies (Britain, France, and Spain) held territory on the new nation's borders. What if one—or all—of them attacked? The colonies had discovered during the revolution that coordination is important when fighting a war. Having thirteen separate state militias, with thirteen separate chains of command, would lead to confusion. They would certainly be less efficient than a unified force.

Besides, invasion from the outside was not the only danger that might call for a military response from the federal government. What if one or more of the states attempted to usurp federal authority, or even used its militia to move against the federal government? Wouldn't the government need some means with which to defend itself?

What if two or more of the states fell to fighting among themselves? Without a military force of its own, how would the federal government be able to keep the peace between them? What if one of the states, acting on its own, provoked a war with some outside power? Suppose a border state sent its militia into Canada, attacking Britain's colonies there? Without an effective federal force to restrain the individual states, might not the whole country be dragged into an unwanted war?

Just as important as the power to make war was the power to make peace. Was each state to decide on its own when it was at war and when it was not? If the country as a whole went to war with some foreign power, could one state make peace for itself without the agreement of the others?

These were not idle concerns. In the few short years the Articles had been in effect, Virginia and Maryland, among others, had made contracts with each other, completely bypassing any federal role. What is more, Georgia had warred on the Indians, apparently without regard to the views of the other states, and then proceeded to sign treaties with them on its own behalf.

For most of the delegates, these concerns outweighed their fears of a federal war power. There seemed to be a general agreement that some kind of federal war power was necessary, but which branch of the new government was to wield it? And under what circumstances?

The new government would have three branches. The legislative branch would have the job of making laws for the new nation and raising the money to finance the government; the executive branch, headed by a president, would enforce the laws made by the legislature; and the judicial branch would act as a mediator between them, and between each of them and the people. Either the executive or legislative branch could exercise the powers involved in making war, but which should? Or should the war powers be divided up between them?

SHOULD THERE BE
A STANDING ARMY?

Under the Articles, the central government had no power to establish an armed force, whether an army or navy, in time of peace. That, the Convention decided, would be changed under the new Constitution.

It seemed logical to most delegates that the legislative branch of government should have the authority to raise and equip armed forces. It was the legislature, after all, which would have to raise the money to finance them. It was the only branch of government which would have the power to levy taxes.

Most of the debate at the Convention about raising armies centered on the question of whether there should be a peacetime army at all. The idea was distasteful to many delegates, who remembered how the British army had been used to intimidate the colonies. Charles Pinckney of South Carolina, however, felt that a military force was necessary. Were no troops "ever to be raised," he asked, "untill [sic] an attack should be made on us?"[3] Might that not be too late?

Despite that concern, Elbridge Gerry of Massachusetts insisted that the people would not accept the Constitution if it didn't include some kind of check against a standing army. He proposed that a limit be imposed on the number of men who could be kept under arms, and suggested a figure of two or three thousand at the most.[4] (George Washington said he agreed, on the condition that any foreign force invading the new country would be limited to a few thousand, too.)

George Mason of Virginia suggested a different kind of limitation—a limitation on Congress's power to appropriate money for the military. This idea was eventually adopted. Congress was finally empowered. "[t]o raise and support armies, but no appropriation of money to that use" could be made for longer than two years.[5] This meant that any federal force would be presumed to be a temporary body. In order to keep it going, Congress would have to recertify it every two years. In effect, this meant it would have to be approved by each succeeding Congress, since a new Congress would be elected every two years. The army, then, would have no independent existence, apart from the will of Congress.

COMMITTING THE NATION TO WAR

Congress was to raise armies and "to provide and maintain a navy," but who would have the direct control over these forces? Who would have the power to commit the nation to the turmoil and the dangers of war?

Those who favored giving that authority to Congress argued that the power was, by its nature, a legislative function. Some claimed that the power to make war or peace was historically regarded to reside in legislatures, others that such powers were usually exercised—in reality if not in theory—by the executive branch, in the form of a monarch. Wasn't it the kings of Europe who traditionally decided when war was, or was not, in the national interest of their countries? They were the ones who ordered their troops into battle. Sometimes they even led them there themselves.

No one at the Convention argued that the United States should have a king. The new country was to have an elected executive authority, a president. But that didn't mean that all powers traditionally exercised by a king—including the power to declare war—had become unnecessary. *Someone* would still have to have authority to decide the questions of war and peace. And if war came, someone would have to have overall authority over the conduct of it. For many of the delegates, it seemed only reasonable that such authority ought to be given to the president.

Unlike the legislature, the president would be a single individual. The president would be able to think, and act, quickly and decisively. This ability could be vital in a time of war. What if the country were suddenly attacked from the outside? Someone had to be able to take charge immediately and order American troops into the field to defend the country.

Even in less drastic circumstances, some delegates argued, Congress would be too large and too slow a body to act effectively. It was expected to meet only once a year. What if a crisis developed when Congress was out of session? In order for the representatives to gather together in one city, many of them would have to travel for days, or even weeks if the weather was bad. They would then be likely to spend even more precious days and weeks in debate before coming to a decision about what to do. Wouldn't it make more sense to put that decision into the hands of a single person?

Others disagreed. They admitted that the legislative might be more slow to act than the executive, but that was not necessarily a bad thing. War was not a desirable state. Most of the delegates thought that it should be undertaken, if at all, only as a last resort. An individual president, they thought, would be more likely to react rashly, in the heat of the moment, than a legislature, which had to take time to convene itself and then to discuss the matter. Time to debate was time to reconsider. Leaving the decision up to the legislature might well prevent wars that might otherwise occur. James Wilson of Pennsylvania, one of the most influential delegates at the Convention, declared it his "object to prevent the President from hurrying us into war." Besides, he argued, they must make sure that no "single man can involve us in (the) distress" of war.[6]

If it *was* desirable for any single individual to have that kind of authority, it seemed to most delegates that the president was the obvious choice. Pierce Butler of South Carolina assured the convention that anyone elected to the presidency would "have all the requisite

George Washington addressing the Constitutional Convention. Delegates discussed what role the president should have in military affairs. Later, Washington became not only the first president, but the first of many with a background of military leadership.

qualities'' to exercise war powers. The president would be unique, the most carefully chosen leader in the land. A special body (the electoral college) would be established for the specific purpose of choosing him. Its members would be selected by all the state legislatures. Surely, they would choose well—as well, at least, as it was possible to choose. If a president chosen after such a painstaking process would not be qualified to exercise war powers, who would? Besides, the president would be the only officeholder in the land to be elected by representatives of all the people, not just those of one state or region. As such, Butler argued, the people could feel sure that the president "will not make war but when the Nation will support it."[7]

Others at the Convention were not so sure. Some, such as Elbridge Gerry, were outraged at the idea of giving such power to one person. Gerry exclaimed that he had "never expected to hear . . . a motion to empower the Executive alone to declare war" in a republic.[8]

The argument against giving the power to wage war to one person had a strong impact on the Convention. It fit the delegates' personal experience. After all, they'd just fought a long and painful war to rid themselves of one monarch who had used his armies against them. They were not eager to see that kind of power put into the hands of a single individual again. The overriding opinion of the delegates was that the power to commit the United States to war should be vested in the legislative branch of the government—specifically, Congress.

TO "MAKE" OR TO "DECLARE"?

In line with what seemed to be the majority opinion of the delegates, a Committee suggested that Congress be given the power to "make war." An amendment passed, however, to change the word "make" to the word "declare." That change of a single word has proved to be a tremendously important one—more important, perhaps, than the delegates realized at the time. In effect, it has served as a justification for presidents asserting a major role in the process of sending troops to war.

In light of the importance this change in wording has taken on since, it's important to examine what we know of why the change was made in the first place. It was introduced by two of the most influential delegates. One was Elbridge Gerry, who spoke out against granting the power to declare war to the president. The other was James Madison, who later became the fourth president of the United States himself. In his notes, Madison describes the proposal as "leaving to the Executive the power to repel sudden attacks."[9] That suggests he may have intended the change only for emergencies, when there would not be time for the legislature to meet. As another delegate put it: "The Executive should have the power to repel and not to commence war."[10]

At least one delegate opposed the change because he thought that the use of "declare" put too much of a limit on congressional authority. On the other hand, George Mason, who opposed granting the power of decision to the executive branch because the president was "not (safely) to be trusted with it," and who was for "clogging rather than facilitating war," still favored the change. He apparently felt, like Madison, that the power it gave to the president was restricted to the case of armed invasion by a foreign power.[11]

Proponents of presidential power, however, argue that the important thing is not what Gerry, Madison, or Mason *intended*. The important thing is what the Convention actually did, and what the Constitution actually says. And on this issue, what it says is only that Congress "shall have the power . . . to declare war." And what that actually means—or *should* actually mean—has been the subject of debate ever since.

The power to declare war is given to Congress in Article I, Section VIII. That same section gives several other war-related powers to Congress, including the authority

> To . . . *grant letters of marque and reprisal, and make rules concerning captures on land and water;*
> *To provide and maintain a navy;*

To make rules for the government and regulation of the land and naval forces;

To provide for calling forth the militia to execute the laws of the Union, suppress insurrections, and repel invasions;

To provide for organizing, arming and disciplining the militia, and for governing such part of them as may be employed in the service of the United States, reserving to the States respectively the appointment of the officers, and the authority of training the militia according to the discipline prescribed by Congress. . . .

The president, however, would not be left out of the process.

THE ROLE OF
COMMANDER-IN-CHIEF

Although the decision to declare war was to be made by Congress, carrying out that decision would fall to the executive. Carrying out the wishes of the legislature was, in any event, an executive function. Under the new system of government, that would mean the president.

Several of the delegates were in favor of dividing up the war powers in some way between Congress and the president. They were determined to put checks on the power of all branches of the new government, because they were worried that one branch would become too powerful. Control over the military was a major aspect of their concern, since the military could be used by tyrants to exert their power. George Mason warned that "the purse and the sword ought never to get into the same hands"[12]—whether those hands were legislative or executive. The purse was to be put in the hands of Congress. The president was left to take the sword.

"The President shall be the Commander-in-Chief of the Army and Navy of the United States," declared Article II, Section II of the Constitution, "and of the militia of the several States when called into the actual service of the United States. . . . "

There seems to have been little, if any, controversy over this provision. There is no record of serious debate on it, despite the fact that it contains no definition of the term "Commander-in-Chief." This lack of controversy at the Convention is surprising in light of the intense controversy which has raged over this function ever since. (It may have been due to the fact that everyone assumed that George Washington would be chosen as the first president.) As we will see in future chapters, the interpretation of this phrase has been at the center of many debates over the war powers of the president.

THE PEACE POWER

One major war-related power remained to be assigned. That was the power to bring wars to an end. Once the country was engaged in military actions, who should have the authority to declare an end to the hostilities?

The delegates recognized the enormous importance of this power. War was a terrible thing, which should be brought to an end as soon as possible. But it was in negotiating for peace that the nation's wealth, prerogatives, and liberties were in danger of being lost. For both these reasons, then, it was vital to put the power to make peace into the most responsible hands possible.

Both houses of Congress had some claim on the power. The House of Representatives, after all, was to have the power to declare war, and it seemed reasonable to give it the power to declare peace as well. If the two powers were put into different hands, there might be a disagreement between them. However, to some delegates, such as Oliver Ellsworth of Connecticut, it made more sense to separate the powers. Ellsworth argued that the considerations involved in exercising the two powers were very different. "There is a material difference," he argued, "between the cases of making *war* and making *peace*. It shd. [sic] be more easy to get out of war, than into it. War is also a simple and overt declaration. peace [sic] attended with intricate and secret negociations [sic]."[13]

Because of the intricacy of negotiations, some argued that the House was too big a body to handle them. They favored giving the peacemaking power to the Senate, which would differ from the House in a number of ways. It would be smaller than the House; its membership would be more stable, since senators would serve longer terms; and senators, unlike House members, would not be elected directly by the people, but by the legislatures of their states. For all these reasons, some delegates assumed that the senators would be more thoughtful and more responsible than the members of the House were likely to be; thus, many delegates favored giving the Senate the power to make treaties of all kinds for the United States. Since wars were usually concluded with the making of a treaty, it was at least as logical to give the peacemaking power to the Senate as to the House.

Still other delegates favored vesting the power in the president. Eventually a compromise was reached (Article II, Section 2) giving the treaty-making power to the president "by and with the advice and consent of the Senate . . . provided two-thirds of the Senators present concur." That power included the power to make treaties of peace.

Madison proposed two amendments to this provision. The first excepted peace treaties from the two-thirds-of-the-Senate requirement. The second empowered two-thirds of the Senators to conclude a peace treaty even if the President disapproved of it. Madison warned that "The President . . . would necessarily derive so much power and importance from a state of war that he might be tempted, if authorized, to impede a treaty of peace."[14] Both amendments were designed to make peace treaties easier to conclude, but both were voted down by the Convention.

Even so, one later president-to-be, Thomas Jefferson, was pleased with the division of war-related powers worked out by the Convention. As he wrote with great satisfaction to James Madison, "We have already given . . . one effectual check to the dog of war, by transferring the power of letting him loose from the Executive to the Legislative body, from those who are to spend to those who are to pay."[15]

The Constitution, then, divides the war powers between Congress and the president. It gives to Congress the powers "to provide for the common defense" and "to declare war." At the same time, it makes the president the Commander-in-Chief of the armed forces, and empowers him (with the advice and consent of the Senate) to make peace.

The result of this division of powers has been a longstanding tension between Congress and the president. The ongoing conflict over the war powers has been one of the great recurring debates in American history.

In the remainder of this book we will explore the issues and arguments raised in this debate. The Constitution forms the background and foundation for the argument, but it cannot finally settle it. Several key terms—such as "declare war" and "Commander-in-Chief"—are left undefined. How they are to be interpreted in practice has been left for actual presidents and Congresses to resolve as they go along. The process is still going on.

DECLARED WARS

The Congress of the United States has declared war five times. In each case, the president was involved in the decision, but in each case he was involved in a different way and to a different extent. The first congressional declaration of war occurred in 1812.

TENSIONS WITH BRITAIN

Tensions had been building up between the United States and Great Britain for many years before they finally burst into war in 1812. In fact, things had never *not* been tense between the young country and its old colonial master. One reason was the lingering resentment brought about by colonialism and the revolution that sprang from it. Another was the desire of many Americans to expand their settlement beyond the new nation's borders.

Almost everywhere, they found themselves blocked and harassed by the British or their allies. To the north was British Canada. To the northwest were Indian tribes who were trading partners of the British. To the south was Florida, a colony of Britain's ally Spain.

Things heated up even further when Britain went to war with France in 1803. Both sides harassed American ships, but the British harassment—which included impressing American seamen—aroused the greatest resentment in the United States. (Impressment was a form of kidnapping, in which sailors were taken prisoner and forced to serve in the British navy.) The most dramatic case of impressment occurred in 1807, when the British ship *Leopard* fired on the American ship *Chesapeake.* After a bloody battle, the *Chesapeake* was forced to give up four men the British claimed were deserters from their navy. Two of them had actually been born in the United States. One of the four was

Commodore Barron (left) *of the U.S.* Chesapeake *offers his sword to the captain of the British ship* Leopard *in 1807. The British proceeded to kidnap four seamen from the American ship.*

later hanged. Altogether, more than 6,200 Americans were eventually impressed into British service. (About 2,500 of them were later jailed, when they refused to fight against the American navy in the War of 1812.)[1]

The high-handed practices of the British navy outraged many Americans, but this was only one of several factors that added to a growing sentiment for war with England. Many frontiersmen believed that an invasion of Canada would solve all of their problems. They were convinced that such an invasion would drive the British out of North America once and for all. Once the British were gone, they thought, they could easily defeat the Indians and sweep westward across the continent. Nor would they be content with Canada and the west. They wanted Florida too. For these "War Hawks," as they came to be called, war with England and Spain would not be a dangerous, unpleasant necessity. It would be welcome. (Ever since, the term "hawk" has been used to describe people who favor a warlike policy.)

Thomas Jefferson, who was president from 1801 to 1809, opposed going to war with England. In his first inaugural address, he called for "peace, commerce, and honest friendship with all nations, entangling alliances with none. . . . "[2] He wanted so badly to avoid war that he called for America to impose a blockade on itself. He helped write the Embargo Act, which forbade Americans to trade with any foreign country whatsoever. He hoped it would remove any possible excuse for either Britain or France to harass American ships, and so remove any further cause of tension.

The Embargo Act was very unpopular. It had the effect of nearly bankrupting the American shipping industry, and many American merchants as well. It was eventually replaced by other laws which put fewer restrictions on American trade. In the meantime, America moved ever closer to war.

It was ironic that it was the president who was

President Thomas Jefferson avoided war with England, but his successor, James Madison, asked for a declaration of war in 1812.

working for peace and a growing number of "War Hawks" in Congress who were calling for war. One of the assumptions at the Constitutional Convention had been that the executive would be more warlike than the legislature. Congress was expected to act as a check on the president. But in this first great test of the war-making powers, it was the other way around.

By the time Jefferson left office in 1809, the battle for peace was already lost. His hand-picked successor, James Madison, favored peace, but many congressmen who had favored Jefferson's policies had been thrown out of office in the elections of 1808 and replaced by "War Hawks." More disappeared in the elections of 1810.

Between the passage of the Constitution and the summer of 1812, five new states were admitted to the

Union. Only the first, Vermont, was in the northeast. All the rest were in the west or south, where sentiment for war was strongest. The elections of 1808 and 1810 shifted the balance. The people were speaking, and they seemed to be saying they wanted war. Madison, meanwhile, was coming around to support the idea himself. By the spring of 1812, his position had changed enough for him to receive the support of his party's "War Hawks" for his reelection bid.[3]

A PRECEDENT IS SET

The Constitution that President Madison had helped to write gave Congress the power to declare war, but it said nothing about how Congress should go about doing it. It seemed to imply, however, that the president would have no direct part in the process. His role would come later, as Commander-in-Chief.

It might have been expected, then, that Congress would have worked out some procedure for itself. And yet, in this first, precedent-setting instance, the president took the lead. In fact, opponents of the war would later argue that he had maneuvered the nation into war in order to further his own expansionist aims.

On June 1, 1812, Madison sent a fateful message to Congress, asking it to declare war on England. The reasons he gave had mostly to do with asserting America's rights to freedom of the seas. Britain, he argued, was already engaging in war against the United States. On the seas, she had fired on American ships and removed American citizens to impress them into her service; in the west, she was encouraging the Indians to attack and kill Americans in her stead. The message suggested that a declaration of war would be nothing more than an announcement that the United States was going to fight back.

President James Madison asked the Congress to declare war on England in 1812. It was the first of only five times in history that the U.S. declared war.

The House passed the declaration three days after receiving the president's message, by a vote of 79 to 49, with the representatives from the south and the frontier voting for war, and those from the northeastern states opposed. The Senate took longer to decide, but on June 17 it, too, voted for war, 19 to 13. On June 18, Madison signed the declaration.[4]

There were several notable aspects of this, the first declaration of war in American history. One was the key role played by the president. Although there was no constitutional requirement (or even specific permission) for him to do so, he was the one who initiated the declaration.

What is more, he was the one who formally laid out the case for war in his message to Congress. He was the one who stated—for the people of the United States and the enemy-to-be alike—the nation's reasons for going to war. Many historians believe that the reasons he gave for the war were less than completely honest.[5] They were almost purely defensive, while in fact, many historians argue, the desire to take over British and Spanish territory played a major part in the decision to declare war—perhaps the largest part. Still, however dishonest the justification for the war may have been, it was the president and not the Congress who spelled it out.

Finally, the president signed the declaration of war, more or less the way he would have signed any routine piece of legislation. It could be argued that by doing so, the president had assumed a veto power over Congress's right to declare war. After all, if his signing was necessary to make the declaration official, a presidential refusal to sign a future declaration might nullify it.

Nonetheless, there was no hint in Madison's message to Congress that he considered himself empowered to make a decision about whether or not to use force against Britain on his own. To the contrary, he acknowledged that the use of military force was a "solemn question which the Constitution wisely confides to the legislative department of the government."[6] In any event, Madison's actions set a precedent for a major presidential role in the act of declaring war. It was a precedent which later presidents would take up, and expand.

Madison also set another precedent, one that later presidents would *not* take up. He joined his troops on the field of battle. The constitutional genius was less than a success as a military leader, however. Shortly before the battle in which Washington, D.C., fell to the British, Madison and his secretary of war rode out on horseback to confer with the American military commander General Winder. Comically, as Madison later wrote, "The unruliness of my horse prevented me from joining in the short conversation that took place."[7]

THE MEXICAN WAR

The war of 1812 was extremely divisive, and the next declared war—the War with Mexico—would be too. James K. Polk, who presided over the war, would prove to be another important figure in the history of the presidential war powers.

The War with Mexico grew out of a dispute over Texas. Texas was clearly a part of Mexico to begin with; however, early in the nineteenth century, American settlers began moving into Texas in large numbers. In 1836, they declared independence and asked to join the United States. In 1845, on the eve of Polk's presidency, Texas was admitted into the Union by a joint resolution of Congress, despite the fact that Mexico still claimed Texas as hers. (Both the Adams and Jackson administrations had offered to buy Texas, but Mexico was no more interested in selling Texas to the United States than the United States was interested in selling Mississippi to Mexico.) The action of the United States in claiming Texas outraged the Mexicans and resulted in widespread sentiment for war with the United States, but the Mexican government was restrained.

Despite the caution of the Mexican government, tensions were high as Polk took office in 1845, and he had no intention of lowering them. The president shared the mood sweeping the United States at that time, a mood expressed by the journalist John L. O'Sullivan: "Texas has been absorbed into the Union in the inevitable fulfillment of the general law which is rolling our population westward . . . [there can be no] doubt of the manifest design of Providence in regard to the occupation of this continent."[8] In other words, the American settlers were destined to move across the

THE GREEDY BOY.

*Many people felt the U.S. was going
too far in claiming all of Texas.*

continent, and absorb it all—all the way out to the
Pacific—into the United States. Polk would not only not
consider giving up the country's claim to Texas, he
wanted New Mexico and California along with it.

In Mexico, anger at the United States was so strong
that the government refused to meet with an ambassador Polk sent to negotiate the sale of territory to the

United States. Even so, the Mexican government was soon ousted by its own people because it seemed too friendly to the United States![9]

Polk, most historians agree, wanted war because war would allow the United States to take what Mexico wouldn't sell—California. At the same time, he realized that the Constitution required him to get a declaration of war from Congress before he could go to war. But Congress was unlikely to grant him one while Mexico confined its protests to words. Consequently, Polk set about trying to provoke the Mexicans.

His method involved an ongoing border dispute. The two countries didn't just disagree about who *owned* Texas, they disagreed about where Texas *was*. The Americans claimed that the southern boundary of Texas was the Rio Grande River, while the Mexicans argued that Texas only extended to the Nueces River, more than 100 miles to the north.[10] (At some points, it was as much as 150 miles north.) Mexico's claim was supported by "all reliable maps and atlases of the period,"[11] but Polk insisted on the weak American claim. He used it to take an action which he felt that Congress would accept and which the Mexican government would have to respond to. He sent a small army, under General Zachary Taylor, into the disputed territory. They camped on the Rio Grande, with guns trained just across the river on the Mexican town of Matamoros. From the American point of view, they were a peace-keeping force camping on American territory, but to the Mexicans they were a hostile army, deep inside Mexico.

Not surprisingly, the Mexican government ordered them to leave. Instead of going, they proceeded to build a fort and blockade the mouth of the Rio Grande, cutting off Matamoros from supplies by sea.[12]

The Mexicans, however, refused to be provoked. Frustrated, Polk decided to ask Congress to declare

President James K. Polk claimed the U.S. had a right to all of the land above the Rio Grande and asked Congress to declare war to establish that right in 1846.

war anyway, using Mexico's refusal to meet with his ambassador (and to pay certain financial claims) to justify the declaration.[13]

But at the last minute, Polk got a much better justification (or excuse) for his request. A band of Mexican soldiers crossed the Rio Grande and killed, wounded, or captured sixty-three American soldiers. On May 11, 1846, Polk sent a message to Congress: "The cup of forbearance has been exhausted. After reiterated menaces, Mexico has passed the boundary of the United States, has invaded our territory and shed American blood upon American soil. . . . [14] War exists, and, notwithstanding all our efforts to avoid it, exists by the act of Mexico herself."[15]

The declaration of war was rushed through the House, with debate limited to only two hours, and the Senate approved it the next day. Supporters argued that haste was needed because Taylor's army might be wiped out at any moment. Opponents pointed out that since the fighting was already under way, the declaration would make no immediate difference to Taylor. Any help sent by Congress would take weeks to get to the Rio Grande. A majority in Congress was outraged by the Mexican action, but others were suspicious. They felt that Polk was trying to railroad them, both to seize California and to help the cause of slavery in the United States. (Texas was a slave state.) The most powerful spokesman for the opponents was Senator Thomas Corwin. "If I were a Mexican," he proclaimed, "I would tell you, 'Have you not room in your own country to bury your dead men? If you come into mine we will greet you with bloody hands, and welcome you to hospitable graves.' "[16] Among other congressional enemies of the war were one ex-president, John Quincy Adams, and one president-to-be, Abraham Lincoln.

Despite their opposition, Congress, pressed by Polk, acted swiftly and decisively. Troops were in the field, and war fever was in the land. The declaration passed 174 to 14 in the House and 40 to 2 in the Senate.[17] Polk's opponents bitterly resented his tactics in laying the ground for the war with Mexico. They considered his representations to Congress in his war message to be out-and-out lies, a fraudulent evasion of the Constitution. In 1848, in fact, the House had second thoughts. It passed a resolution stating that the war with Mexico had been "unnecessarily and unconstitutionally begun by the President of the United States."[18] (Both Adams and Lincoln voted for it.)

During the war itself, Polk took much of the responsibility for directing American military efforts from the White House. He often complained, in fact, that he could not take more. There was an ongoing conflict between Congress and the president over how much control of military affairs the president should have. "My situation is most embarrassing," he complained at one point. "I am held responsible for the war, and I am required to entrust the chief command of the army to a general in whom I have no confidence."[19] The choice of a field commander was not his only bone of contention with Congress. He consistently felt that Congress restrained his efforts to direct the conduct of the war. "To add to my embarrassment," he complained at another time, "and it does greatly do so, Congress does not strengthen the Executive arm . . . with a large nominal majority in both Houses, I am practically in a minority."[20]

Polk clearly felt that he could direct the war better than either Congress or his military commanders. Even so, his action seems to show that he accepted the assumption that Congress had the ultimate power to direct him—even in his role as Commander-in-Chief—if it chose to do so.

THE SPANISH–AMERICAN WAR

As we have seen, the role of the president in each of American's first two declared wars was a controversial one. As foreign policy expert Adolf A. Berle has explained: "The thrust of the accusation against [both Madison and Polk] was that, in both cases, the President had manipulated events to produce a condition of affairs in which the Congress had little alternative."[21] It had to declare war. The situation when it came to America's third declaration of war was almost the reverse, with Congress and the press manipulating the president toward war with Spain.

The issue was (or seemed to be) Spain's island colony of Cuba. Spain ruled the impoverished little island with a stern hand, and there was a good deal of sympathy in America when an uprising took place there against Spanish rule. Spanish reaction was harsh and bloody. Some American newspapers, particularly William Randolph Hearst's New York *Journal* and Joseph

President William McKinley asked Congress to declare war on Spain in 1898.

Pulitzer's New York *World*, played the story for all it was worth. In editorials, they called for America to help the neighboring island in its fight for independence.

The call met with agreement among many politicians, including Senator Henry Cabot Lodge and the assistant secretary of the Navy, Theodore Roosevelt. They saw a chance for the United States to become an important imperialist power. They knew the Spanish navy was weak, and they believed the United States could easily wrest Spain's North American colonies away from her. Cuba, they felt, could provide the spark to set off the necessary war.

President McKinley, on the other hand, was apparently reluctant. He sympathized with Cuba but didn't see the need for war. He did, however, send a United

States battleship, the *Maine*, to Havana when a riot endangered Americans there.[22] On February 15, 1898, the *Maine* blew up in Havana harbor and more than 260 Americans were killed. Although there was no proof of who (or even what) caused the explosion, many people blamed Spain. Almost immediately, Roosevelt ordered the Asiatic Squadron of the U.S. Navy to Hong Kong, where it would be in position for a quick attack on the Spanish fleet in the Philippines.[23]

McKinley remained cautious, despite the growing clamor for war, but made several demands on Spain. By April 9, Spain had agreed to virtually all of them (except to free Cuba outright). Nonetheless, the pressure for war continued. Finally, in the words of historian George Fort Milton, McKinley "weakly yielded to the war party."[24] He asked Congress for authority to use force in Cuba. Congress wasn't just happy to oblige, it was eager to go even further. On April 19, it declared Cuba free and independent, and ordered Spain to leave the island. In response, Spain broke off diplomatic relations with the United States on April 21. Four days later, Congress declared war, proclaiming that a state of war had existed from the moment Spain broke off relations.[25]

The United States won the easy victory everyone expected. And the victory made Washington a world power, just as Roosevelt, Hearst, and Lodge had wanted. She took possession of three Spanish colonies—Guam, Puerto Rico, and the Philippines—giving her a major, even dominant role in the trade with the Orient.[26] One ironic result of this new prominence in world affairs was a strengthened presidency, since foreign relations was largely an executive function. As historian Arthur M. Schlesinger, Jr., has pointed out, this war the president didn't want and Congress did ended up fattening presidential power at Congress's expense.[27]

WOODROW WILSON
AND WORLD WAR I

Both world wars in this century were declared by Congress. In both cases, however, the presidents involved—Woodrow Wilson and Franklin D. Roosevelt—used the office of president to steer the country in the direction of war.

Wilson started out trying to avoid war at almost any cost, but it was his insistence on American freedom of the seas that ultimately made war with Germany almost inevitable. When Germany went to war with Britain and France in the summer of 1914, Wilson announced that the United States would remain neutral. "We must be neutral in fact as well as name," he said. "(W)e must be impartial in thought as well as in action, must put a curb upon our sentiments."[28] But neutrality proved hard to maintain when Germany announced (on Feb. 4, 1915) that she would sink any ships attempting to trade with the Allies.

Wilson responded that the United States would hold Germany accountable for any sinking of an American ship. Then, when a German submarine sank the British passenger liner *Lusitania* on May 7, 1915, killing more than 100 Americans among the 1,198 people lost, Wilson responded angrily again.[29] Nonetheless, Germany went ahead with a policy of sinking merchant ships without warning. In 1916, Wilson warned the Germans that if they continued that policy, the United States would sever relations. The Germans backed down temporarily, but then returned to unrestricted submarine warfare in January of 1917.

By that time, Wilson had backed himself—and the United States—into a corner. He had threatened war if Germany sank American ships, and the Germans intended to do just that. That February, Wilson asked

American anger at the sinking of the Lusitania *in 1915—with the loss of over 100 American lives— sparked public sentiment for war with Germany.*

After first trying to avoid it, President Woodrow Wilson finally led the U.S. into World War I.

Congress for the authority to arm American merchant ships to defend themselves. There was a great deal of both public and congressional support for the move. In fact, there was a growing sentiment for war. But peace-oriented senators launched a filibuster to block the authorization. Wilson went ahead and armed the ships anyway.[30] On March 18, the Germans sank three American ships, and on April 2, Wilson asked Congress to declare war. It did, on April 6, 1917.[31]

Wilson had committed the United States in his threats to Germany, and had armed the merchant ships without congressional authority. But it is debatable whether these actions, which were eventually ratified by Congress, effectively increased the war powers of the presidency. The actions of Wilson's administration during the war, however, certainly increased the scope of governmental power on the home front. As historians Allan Nevins and Henry Steele Commager have pointed out, "Wilson proved one of the greatest of war presidents, controlling every aspect of the war effort. . . ."[32]

Wilson mobilized the country for war as it had never been mobilized before. A national draft was instituted. Wilson's administration took virtual control of American industry, communications, and transportation. It established a War Industries Board that controlled government purchasing, a Food Administration to regulate food production, and an Aircraft Production Board, among other agencies designed to promote the war effort. However, while this enormous—and enormously successful—mobilization can be seen as an expansion of executive power, it was not carried out over the opposition of Congress. Although some of these agencies were originally established by presidential order, they were all eventually authorized by Congress as well.[33]

ROOSEVELT AND WORLD WAR II

Interestingly, President Franklin D. Roosevelt, who guided America through its bloodiest foreign war, was one of the most restrained of all American presidents in his use of the war powers during his early years in office. In fact, throughout the first two and one-half terms of his presidency—until the eve of America's entry into World War II—American troops had been sent ashore in hostile circumstances only twice. Both involved extremely limited actions to protect American interests in China.[34]

When war broke out in Europe in 1939, however, Roosevelt was convinced that American interests required an Allied victory. If the United States' fellow democracies in Europe fell to the Nazis and Fascists, he believed, she would be alone and vulnerable. But the American people as a whole did not agree with the president.[35] They had had enough of fighting wars in Europe back in 1917, and they wanted no part of this new one. Roosevelt was a politician, and he was not about to take the country into war without the people of the country behind him. He proceeded to use the power of his position as president—the power his relative Theodore had referred to as the "bully pulpit"—to push and persuade the country into aiding the Allies and preparing for war herself.

To begin with, the president declared a "limited national emergency," and raised the numbers of men in the Army and National Guard. He asked Congress to revise neutrality legislation that forbade the United States from selling arms to a country engaged in war. Congress agreed, changing the law so that arms could be sold on a direct cash basis. This change allowed for sale to both the Allies *and* Germany, and so could be defended as being in line with America's policy of neu-

President Franklin D. Roosevelt led the U.S. into—and during— World War II.

trality. In fact, the policy favored the Allies because Great Britain, with one of the most powerful navies in Europe, could easily buy and ship military supplies across the Atlantic, while Germany could not.[36]

Arguing that it was necessary for defense of the Western Hemisphere in case the war should spread, Roosevelt persuaded Congress to approve the buildup of virtually every branch of the military. "We will extend to the opponents of force the material resources of this nation; and, at the same time . . . speed up the use of these resources in order that we . . . may have equipment and training equal to the task of any emergency."[37] In all of that, Roosevelt acted openly, and with the approval of Congress, although some people doubted he really meant it when he said "this country is not going to war."[38] Perhaps his most controversial action, however, was the transfer of 50 mothballed destroyers to Britain in exchange for leases on military bases in the West Indies, Newfoundland, and Bermuda. Most historians agree that from that moment on, the declared American policy of neutrality was a myth. Roosevelt secretly transferred some U.S. Army and Navy equipment, including airplanes, to the Allies. After these actions had been made public, he asked for, and got, a Lend-Lease Bill from Congress that authorized him to "sell, transfer, exchange, lease, lend" any military articles to any country "whose defense the President deems vital to the defense of the United States." Using this authority, the United States eventually transferred some 50 billion dollars' worth of supplies and equipment to the Allies.[39]

Even though he was convinced that America should enter the war as soon as possible, in order to save the European democracies from fascism and thus protect America, Roosevelt refrained from asking for a declaration of war because he knew that most Americans would not accept it. One poll, for example, taken just a month before Pearl Harbor, showed that only one in five Americans favored going to war with Germany.[40]

The lack of a declaration of war didn't stop the president from taking action altogether, however. And some of the actions he took strained the accepted limits of his authority. He announced that the United States was taking first Greenland and then Iceland under its protection. He seized German, Japanese, and Italian ships in American ports, and froze those countries' assets in American banks.

Finally, after there had already been one skirmish between a U.S. Navy ship and a German submarine, Roosevelt ordered the Navy to fire on any and all German U-boats sighted. The order was given in September, but it wasn't until November that Congress amended the Neutrality Act to authorize such actions in defense of American Lend Lease shipments.[41] Despite such actions (or because of them) a number of American merchant ships were sunk by submarines.[42] And still the people did not want the United States to go to war.

Then, on December 7, 1941, the Japanese attacked an American naval base at Pearl Harbor, Hawaii. The next day, with the country aroused at last, Roosevelt asked for and got a war resolution from Congress. Although the great majority of Americans had been opposed to war only a few days before, there was only one dissenter in the entire Congress.[43]

The 1941 bombing of Pearl Harbor gave Roosevelt his opportunity to ask Congress to declare war.

Some historians have been suspicious of the strength of this turnaround and believe that Roosevelt used his position as president to provoke the attack in some way, getting the Japanese to arouse American public opinion for him. Others argue that although he may not have provoked the attack, he knew, or should have known, that something like it was coming. They say he deliberately left the American forces unprepared in order to make the attack seem more terrible when it did come. Others maintain that there is no good evidence for either claim.[44] In any case, there is no doubt that once the attack occurred, majority opinion— both in Congress and among the public—favored going to war.

In World War II, as in World War I, there was a massive mobilization of resources on the home front, directed by the executive department of government and generally approved by Congress. Two of the more dramatic and controversial exercises of executive power: the president's seizing of over sixty plants and industries involved in labor controversies, in order to keep them operating for the war effort; and the forced removal of over seventy thousand American citizens of Japanese ancestry from the west coast, who were then interned in government-run camps in order to prevent them from aiding a feared Japanese invasion.[45] The second of these actions was widely supported at the time but has since been almost universally condemned as a slur on the loyalty of Japanese-Americans, not one of whom was ever found guilty of any disloyal action during the war.

THE MAN WHO HOLDS THE POWER—
LINCOLN AND THE CIVIL WAR

Probably no president before or since has exercised the war powers as broadly and decisively as Abraham Lincoln—and he did it in a war that was never declared by Congress.

Congress was not in session on April 12, 1861, when Fort Sumter was fired on by the military forces of South Carolina. Rather than call it into session, Lincoln immediately sent help to the fort, knowing very well that his act would result in open hostilities. And he did more. He called for new troops (under an act from 1795) to be used as *posses comitatus*—citizens who would help the duly authorized officials enforce the laws. He also increased the size of the regular army and navy, something that had always been considered a congressional prerogative. He ordered a naval blockade put on southern ports. He gave his military commanders the authority to suspend the constitutional right to a writ of *habeas corpus* whenever "necessary." And finally, he ordered the Department of the Treasury to provide a great deal of money to pay for all these war measures, despite the fact that only Congress had the constitutional authority to appropriate funds.[1]

Lincoln was aware when he did all these things that the Constitution did not directly give him the power to do them. Yet, he argued, "By necessary implication, when rebellion or invasion comes . . . I think the man whom, for the time, the people have, under the Constitution, made the commander-in-chief of their army and navy, is the man who holds the power and bears the responsibility" of using it.[2]

Essentially, Lincoln's argument was that this case was something different in American history. What was involved was not protecting Americans abroad, or defending American ships on the high seas, or attacking a foreign nation. This was an insurrection on American soil.

The last point was crucial to his defense of what he was doing. "If I be wrong on this question of constitutional power," he wrote, "my error lies in believing that certain proceedings are constitutional when, in cases of rebellion or invasion, the public safety requires them, which would not be constitutional when, in absence of rebellion or invasion, the public safety does not require them: in other words, that the Constitution is not in its application in all respects the same in cases of rebellion or invasion involving the public safety, as it is in times of profound peace and public security."[3] He argued this despite the fact that Article 1, Section 8 of the Constitution gives Congress, not the president, the power of "calling forth" the militia to "suppress insurrections."

In fact, Lincoln argued that in such times he could do *more than* Congress could. "I conceive that I may . . . do things on military grounds which cannot constitutionally be done by the Congress."[4] If a president uses the extraordinary power he has in such cases "justly, the . . . people will probably justify him; if he abuses it, he is in their hands to be dealt with by all the modes they have reserved to themselves in the Constitution."[5]

President Abraham Lincoln led the nation into the Civil War without ever asking Congress to declare war on the Confederacy.

Lincoln later invited Congress to ratify some of his actions, but usually after he had already taken them. What he had really done, as Marcus Raskin among others have pointed out, was to take the power to act as he did and then to dare Congress to impeach him.[6] What Congress did instead, when it met later in 1861 (well after the war was underway) was to vote the president virtually unlimited power to meet whatever emergencies might arise.[7] (At this point, of course, it was a solely northern Congress.) War was not declared, however—presumably because there was no foreign nation on which to declare war. Although the southern states were trying to secede from the Union, the federal government's position was that they had no right to do so. Consequently, they were not a foreign country.

THE PRIZE CASES

The so-called *Prize Cases* were the most important legal test of Lincoln's war powers to reach the courts. When they were decided in 1863, the courts tended to agree with Congress in "justifying" the president. The crisis the nation faced overrode all other concerns. The *Prize Cases* were challenges to a proclamation made on April 19, 1861, that ordered the blockade of southern ports a week after the first shots on Fort Sumter. The blockade was put into effect immediately, but it was not confirmed by Congress until August 6. The plaintiffs argued that the proclamation was illegal under the generally accepted "laws of nations." (The "laws of nations" was a concept embodied in the Constitution.) A blockade was an act of war, and only the duly constituted power of a national state could impose one. Only Congress had the war power. The Constitution never "contemplated . . . that the President should be dictator, and all constitutional government be at an end, whenever he should think that 'the life of the nation' is in danger." The Supreme Court, however, disagreed. The president, declared Justice Grier, speaking for the Court, had had to meet the rebellion "in the shape it presented itself, without waiting for Congress to baptize it with a name, and no name given to it by him or them could change the fact."[8] But the key fact in the *Prize* decision was the fact that Congress had, finally, ratified the blockade.

Although such ratification may not even have been necessary "under the circumstances," the court said, "it is plain that if the President had in any manner assumed powers which it was necessary should have the authority or sanction of Congress, that on the well-known principle of law, '*omnis ratihabitio retrotrahitur et mandato equiparatur*,' this ratification has operated to perfectly cure the defect."[9]

Despite the fact that the Court approved the blockade, it did not approve some of the president's other actions, which it considered invasions of Congress's power. Significantly, it reaffirmed that "By the Constitution, Congress alone has the power to declare a national or foreign war."[10]

In another case, the courts were much less supportive of a presidential action. Lincoln had signed a military order commanding General John A. Dix to seize and stop publication of two major New York newspapers, the *World* and the *Journal*, which had printed false and apparently malicious information about the government. After three days, the order was lifted, but the governor of New York had Dix arrested. The general pleaded that he had only been following the orders of his Commander-in-Chief, and that he could not be held liable for doing so because of the Indemnity Act passed by Congress in 1863. The Supreme Court, however, ruled the act unconstitutional. Dix's case was put to a grand jury, but the grand jury failed to return an indictment, and so the constitutionality of the president's order was never tested before the Supreme Court.[11]

During the war, the Supreme Court dodged the issue of whether the president's suspension of habeas corpus and imposition of martial law had been constitutional. After the war, however, it cast doubt on the constitutionality of some of Lincoln's actions in a case known as *ex parte Milligan*.[12]

THE EMANCIPATION
PROCLAMATIONS

Lincoln's most controversial—and most far-reaching—use of the war powers was his freeing of the slaves. The preliminary Emancipation Proclamation was issued on September 22, 1862, and the final one on New

Year's Day, 1863. The proclamations had effect only in those areas which were, at that time, in rebellion against the government. Slavery remained in place in those areas of the South which were already under Union control.[13] However, most importantly, they declared freedom of the slaves a major goal of the war, something it hadn't been before.

From the modern perspective, freeing the slaves seems such an obvious and morally necessary thing to do that it is hard to understand why it was not a major goal of the federal government from the beginning. Most of the so-called civilized countries of the world had abandoned slavery long before 1861. Britain, for example, had outlawed the slave trade in 1807. Lincoln's Republican party had been founded largely to halt the expansion of slavery in the United States; and Lincoln himself personally disapproved of slavery, although before the rebellion he thought it only reasonable that slaveowners should be paid for their slaves if they were set free by government order.[14] And yet, until the Emancipation Proclamation it was by no means certain whether a Union victory would result in freedom for the slaves.

As president, Lincoln's main concern—some say his only concern—was to preserve the Union. He was determined to do whatever would win the most support for the Union cause. Although many of the Union's strongest supporters were abolitionists who wanted an immediate end to slavery, many were not. Many northerners as well as southerners believed that the federal government had no right to tell the states they couldn't have slavery if they wanted to. Besides, some northerners argued, slaves were private property, and the government had no right to confiscate the private property of law-abiding citizens—those not engaged in rebellion against the government. Freeing the slaves might lose conservative support for the war in the

Lincoln issued the final Emancipation Proclamation on January 1, 1863, an event celebrated some two decades later by the owners of this Richmond, Virginia, store.

North. It would certainly anger the border states, who practiced slavery but sympathized with the Union. And it would inflame white southerners even further. It was the president's early judgment that to free the slaves would only hurt the Union's cause.

He was not about to let his subordinates free them either. Major General John Charles Frémont (who in 1856 had been the first Republican presidential candidate) was the military commander in the Department of the West in 1862. An abolitionist at heart, Frémont decided to punish the rebellious slaveholders of Missouri by freeing their slaves. Lincoln not only overruled Frémont's order, he removed him from his military command. In doing so, he declared that he, and he alone, would decide "whether it be competent for me, as Commander-in-Chief of the Army and Navy, to declare the slaves of any State or States free."[15]

Having reserved the right to declare slaves free, he decided to do just that the next year. Although the Emancipation Proclamation had enormous moral and social significance, it was not done for moral or social reasons, but for military ones. It was, in fact, an act of military desperation. As Lincoln himself expressed the situation: "We have about played our last card, and must change our tactics or lose the game."[16]

On the advice of his secretary of war, he waited to issue the proclamation till after a Union military victory would make it seem less desperate than it was. The chance came when McClellan's forces defeated Lee's at Sharpsburg, in what is usually referred to as the Battle of Antietam, on September 17, 1863. The first proclamation was issued five days later.[17]

Lincoln claimed the right to free the slaves in the rebel states under "the power in me vested as Commander-in-Chief of the Army and Navy of the United States in time of actual armed rebellion against the authority and Government of the United States, and as a fit and necessary war measure for suppressing said rebellion."[18] William Howard Taft, a former president himself and later the Chief Justice of the Supreme Court, agreed with Lincoln's argument. He described the proclamation as "an act of the Commander-in-Chief justified by military necessity to weaken the enemies of the Nation and suppress . . . rebellion."[19]

As expected, the proclamation outraged the South, but it also, as hoped, fired up the will of northern abolitionists. What's more, it helped win the support of Britain for the Union blockade of southern ports that was depriving her of the cotton she needed for her textile industry.[20]

Although emancipation was proclaimed as a war measure, the freed slaves were to be free "then, thenceforward and forever." And when a later proclamation was issued on December 8, 1863, setting out the conditions under which rebellious states would be accepted back into the Union, one of the conditions was that they would have to recognize and accept the emancipation of their slaves.[21] The end of slavery was made final by the passage of the Thirteenth Amendment to the Constitution of the United States in 1865.

A GREAT EXCEPTION?

It has been argued that Lincoln's sweeping use of the war powers should be regarded as a kind of great exception to the constitutional rules limiting presidential power. As we have seen, Lincoln argued as much himself.

The Civil War was itself a kind of great exception in American history. Both the war and the circumstances surrounding it were unique. There was no foreign enemy to fight, only Americans, and the issue at stake was a fundamental one. It wasn't a question of a national interest in the usual sense. Nor was it a revolution, in which the issue would have been who would run the country, or how it should be run. The issue, as Lincoln saw it, was whether the United States would continue to exist as a country—period. The only constitutional question that finally mattered, when it came to deciding that question, was whether there would be a Constitution at all.

For this reason, it can be argued that Lincoln's actions should not be considered a precedent for other presidents to follow. Nonetheless, a number of later presidents (and their supporters) have pointed to Lincoln's example to justify their own claims to special powers. Ultimately, every president sees his own circumstances, as well as the threats to the country he (and someday she) has to face, as unique. How, they might ask, can rights and prerogatives available to one president be denied to others? From the point of view of those who support presidential power, at least, it has been a powerful argument.

UNDECLARED WARS
AND OTHER ACTIONS

Presidents Wilson and Roosevelt were attacked for using their powers to maneuver America into the two world wars. However, as legal expert Raoul Berger has pointed out, although their actions were clearly "provocative and might have drawn the nation into war . . . they were still short of 'war'." Neither of them "sent combat troops to engage in actual hostilities on foreign soil until Congress declared war."[1] Nonetheless, Wilson sent troops to Mexico before the First World War, and Roosevelt came close when he ordered American ships to fire on German U-boats whether or not they fired first.

But there have been many other cases in which presidents *have* used their power to send troops to engage in "actual hostilities on foreign soil."

PROTECTION OF AMERICAN
LIVES AND PROPERTY

Until fairly recently, as historian Edward S. Corwin has pointed out, most instances of presidentially ordered military actions were "efforts to protect the definite rights of persons and property against impending violence, and were defended on that ground as not amounting to acts of war."[2] Thomas Jefferson announced the first of these "efforts" in the first of his annual messages to Congress, informing it that he had sent "a small squadron of frigates" to the Mediterranean because of the pirates attacking American ships there.[3]

The United States had signed treaties with some of the small Barbary states along the coast of North Africa, promising protection for American ships trading in the area. (It was the kind of "protection" some small businesses pay to the mob.) But the pirates continued to harass the ships and even to take American seamen as prisoners, and the United States had been forced to pay over half a million dollars in ransom for the captured sailors.

By the time Jefferson notified Congress, the ships had already left, but Congress did not object. Indeed, it passed a number of resolutions over the next several years authorizing this kind of presidential action.

Eventually, the *Pasha* of one of the Barbary states, Tripoli (in what is now Libya), threw out his treaty and declared war on the United States, allowing him to prey freely on American ships. Even then, Congress did not declare war in response but let the president direct the defense of the ships on his own authority. Jefferson continued to do so throughout his term, and his successor, Madison, oversaw a similar campaign in 1815.[4]

(The very first use of American troops abroad had occurred under President John Adams, from 1798 to 1800, in what was known as the Undeclared Naval War with France. The "war" included several sea battles between American and French ships, as well as limited land actions.[5] Despite the fact it was never declared, however, the "war" was authorized by Congress, and

— 73 —

in advance. Before ordering military action, the president called Congress into a special session "to consult and determine such measures as in their wisdom shall be deemed meet for the safety and welfare of the . . . United States."[6] As a result, Congress passed legislation that the Supreme Court later ruled amounted to a kind of declaration of "imperfect," or partial, war.[7])

Jefferson's Barbary Wars were two dramatic instances of American military intervention to protect American lives and property (including trading rights) abroad. There have been scores of others since, in many countries all over the globe. Some, like Adams' Undeclared War, have been specifically authorized by Congress in advance; some have been approved after the fact; and others have been either formally ignored by Congress or repudiated by it. What follows is a brief list, describing only a small percentage of these instances.[8]

From 1822 to 1825, American forces landed on Cuba several times to hunt down pirates. On one occasion, they burned down a pirate headquarters there.

In 1827, naval forces conducted similar actions in Greece.

In 1832, Americans landed on the Falkland Islands, off the coast of Argentina, to protect the property and persons of American seal hunters. The next year they landed in Argentina itself.

In 1843, both sailors and marines went ashore at Canton, China, to protect an American trading post there.

In 1855, American forces landed in Nicaragua to protect Americans during political disturbances.

In 1854, similar landings took place in both China and Nicaragua. (There would be many more such landings in both China and Nicaragua.)

Instances like these happened again and again throughout the nineteenth century. The turn of the century (1900) saw one of the largest of all such actions, when President William McKinley sent five thousand troops to join in an international force to protect Americans and other foreigners in China during the Boxer Rebellion. After that uprising had been put down, the United States continued to maintain a military force at its legation in Peking for more than thirty years.

In this century, the protection of American lives or property has been the stated reason for military actions in such varied places as Syria (1903), Korea (1904–1905), Turkey (1912), Palestine (1948), Cyprus (1974), and Lebanon (1972 and 1982), as well as in most of the countries of the Western Hemisphere. More recently, the protection of the lives of American students was one of the chief reasons given by President Reagan for the American invasion of Grenada in 1983.

Sometimes these instances have been very brief, consisting of a single landing or engagement. Sometimes they have gone on, though often without actual combat, for many years. In addition to the Peking legation guard mentioned above, for example, there were American forces in China from 1912 to 1941, in Nicaragua from 1926 to 1933, and in Panama from 1903 to 1914.

PROTECTING AND ASSERTING AMERICAN "INTERESTS"

Presidents have often ordered military actions to further broadly defined national interests of various kinds, whether geographical, commercial, or ideological.

The many Indian wars of the nineteenth century were undertaken for what might be called geographical reasons. They were fought primarily to obtain lands in which the country could stretch westward, and to protect American settlers as they moved into them.

The Barbary Wars were undertaken to protect

American commercial interests as much as to protect American seamen. Similar motives caused American naval forces, under Commodore Matthew Perry, to be sent to Japan in 1853 and 1854.

The Japanese coast was dangerous, and many American ships and sailors had washed up on Japanese shores. Most of them were soon released, but some reported cruel treatment at the hands of the Japanese. The American government was angered by these reports, but indignation was not the only reason to send the navy to Japan.

Japan was potentially a rich source of coal for American steamships trading with the Orient, and a possible market for American goods as well. So Perry was instructed not just to get assurance of decent treatment for Americans shipwrecked in Japan, but to get agreements allowing Americans to trade in Japanese ports and to establish a coal depot in the country. When Perry arrived, with an impressive show of American naval power, the Japanese offered several concessions.[9] Nonetheless, Perry actually put troops ashore on the Japanese islands of Bonin and Ryukyu, forcing the ruler of Okinawa to grant the United States a coal concession.[10] The Bonins were returned to Japanese control in 1861, but the United States continued to assert its commercial interests in the area for many years.[11]

Although commercial interests were also involved in the American occupation of the Philippine Islands after the Spanish–American War, they were not the only interests involved. Many Americans wanted the United States to take a role as an imperial power in the world, and they saw the Philippines as the foundation for an American empire. President McKinley, however, claimed a more spiritual motive. He described his decision about what to do with the Philippines this way:

"I thought first we would take only [the Philippine island of] Manila; then Luzon; then other islands perhaps, also. I walked the floor of the White House night after night until midnight . . . I went down on my knees and prayed Almighty God for light and guidance more than one night. And one night it came to me this way—I don't know how it was, but it came . . . there was nothing left for us to do but to take them all, and to educate the Filipinos, and uplift and civilize and Christianize them, and by God's grace to do the best we could with them . . . and then I went to bed, and went to sleep, and slept soundly.''[12]

McKinley's inspiration was a graphic example of the personal nature of a presidential decision—and of presidential power.

Taking the Philippines from Spain proved to be little problem. Spain ceded them, along with Guam and Puerto Rico, to the United States for twenty million dollars. But taking them from the Filipinos proved more difficult. It required an undeclared war that went on for two years, which was considerably longer than the Spanish–American War itself had lasted. It was a war fought with a viciousness previously unkown in American conflicts. Before it was ended—by presidential proclamation on July 4, 1902—more than forty-two hundred Americans and twenty thousand Filipinos had been killed.[13]

McKinley's successor, Theodore Roosevelt, was determined to build a canal connecting the Atlantic and Pacific oceans. The most logical place for it seemed to be the Isthmus of Panama, which belonged at that time to the nation of Colombia. Roosevelt offered terms to the Colombians which they rejected as unacceptable. The president was thinking of going ahead, seizing the Isthmus and building the canal anyway, when a group of Panamanians revolted against Colombian rule. The revolution, it turned out, was led by an engineer working for a French company negotiating to build the canal for the United States.[14] Some people suspected Roosevelt of having a hand in planning the revolution, but

This painting shows the future twenty-sixth president, Theodore Roosevelt, leading his Rough Riders on horseback during the Spanish-American War. Roosevelt's military experiences influenced his presidential style.

there is no proof of that. What the president did do, however, was send the U.S. cruiser *Nashville* to Panama to make sure the revolution would succeed.[15]

Roosevelt was proud of his action, and of the fact that he hadn't asked Congress for authorization in advance. "If I *had* followed traditional conservative methods," he bragged later, "I would have submitted a dignified state paper of probably two hundred pages to Congress and the debate would be going on yet. But I took the Canal Zone and let Congress debate, and while the debate goes on the canal does also."[16]

RETALIATION

In 1824, American naval forces, led by Commodore David Porter, attacked the town of Fajardo on the then Spanish-held island of Puerto Rico and forced an apology for insults to American officers. In 1832, forces descended on the town of Quallah Battoo in Sumatra to punish it for actions committed by pirates based there against American ships. These were two early acts of American military retaliation for offenses against American interests, or the American flag, abroad. There have been many others since.

Although one reason for retaliation is the protection of American interests—by deterring the countries or individuals involved from committing hostile actions in the future—retaliation has several aspects that distinguish it from other military or police actions.

Acts of retaliation are usually brief and specific. They are rarely military engagements in the sense of two armed forces fighting each other. And they often involve activities that would not be considered acceptable under ordinary circumstances, such as direct attacks on civilian, rather than military, targets. They also involve the emotional element of national pride.

Perhaps because of this emotional element, military retaliation often seems out of all proportion to the acts that prompt it. One example of this lack of proportion took place in Nicaragua during the presidency of Franklin Pierce, the same president who oversaw Admiral Perry's taking of the Bonins.

There was a civil disturbance in the coastal town of San Juan del Norte, or Greytown, on the southwest coast of Nicaragua in 1854. During the course of the trouble, a bottle was thrown at an American diplomat. In response to this relatively minor act of violence, an American warship, the *Cyane*, was sent to Nicaragua. It sailed to Greytown harbor and its captain demanded an apology for the claimed insult to the United States. Literally under the guns of the American warship, the Nicaraguans refused. The *Cyane* opened fire and destroyed the town.[17]

The most dramatic exception to the rule that retaliation is usually brief and specific was the American intervention in Mexico under President Wilson. The Mexican revolution, which started in 1910, resulted in a confused situation in Mexico, in which several factions battled for power. In 1913, President Wilson offered to mediate between the two most powerful of these factions, one led by Victoriano Huerta and the other by Venustiano Carranza. Huerta refused. When Huerta later became the dictator of Mexico, Wilson proceeded to do what he could to undermine him diplomatically, and even offered to send military help to Carranza. The help was refused, but Carranza asked for, and got, the right to buy arms from the United States.

The situation was tense between the United States and Mexican governments in April 1914, when some American sailors on shore at Tampico, Mexico, were arrested by Mexican forces. They were quickly released, but Admiral Henry Mayer demanded that the Mexicans fire off a 21-gun salute in honor of the American flag. This the Mexicans refused to do.[18]

President Wilson quickly asked for (and got) authority from Congress to enforce his demands on the Mexican government for "unequivocal amends for affronts and indignities committed against the United States."[19] He used this authority to order the navy to capture the Mexican city of Veracruz, which it did on April 21 and 22, at a cost of 126 Mexican and 19 American lives.[20] Control of the port at Veracruz meant that the United States was able to cut off the Mexican government's supplies of arms from Germany as well as its cash income from foreign trade. As a result, Huerta's government fell to Carranza. Wilson had succeeded in toppling the Mexican government.[21]

The troubles between the United States and Mexico didn't end there, however. Another Mexican revolutionary leader, named Pancho Villa, who controlled much of northern Mexico, turned against Carranza. When Wilson recognized Carranza's government in 1915, Villa was angry. He made several raids across the border into New Mexico in 1916, killing Americans and attempting to stir up trouble between the United States and the Carranza government.

That March, Wilson ordered General John J. Pershing and a force of six thousand men across the border to hunt down Villa. They chased after him for some three hundred miles into Mexico, managing to offend the Mexican government despite its own problems with Villa. There were skirmishes between U.S. and Mexican forces, and Carranza ordered the U.S. soldiers to leave Mexican soil. Under Wilson's orders, they refused. Although they never caught Villa, they stayed in Mexico until February 1917.[22]

The practice of isolated retaliation, apart from larger military conflicts, largely disappeared from U.S. policy after the Second World War.[23] The Reagan administration, however, revived the practice in Lebanon in 1982.

The president ordered 1,200 Marines (later joined by several hundred others) to Lebanon in September 1982. They were reportedly there as part of a multinational force to keep order while an embattled Lebanese government attempted to reassert its control over the country. There was, however, much controversy within the United States over the true purpose of sending them there.[24] In any event, when the Marines came under fire from Syrian installations (and Lebanese factions), American planes began staging air raids in retaliation. (The Marines themselves, having been put in the role of peacekeepers, were forbidden to take part in combat.)

The worst attack on the Marines came on October 23, 1983, when a truck bomb hit a Marine barracks at

Lebanon, 1983

the Beirut airport and killed 241 Marines while most of them were asleep. It was not until September 29, 1983, in advance of that attack, that Congress passed a resolution authorizing the president to keep the Marines in Lebanon for another eighteen months if necessary. The resolution was widely interpreted as a show of American unity and determination not to run in the face of the attack on the Marines.

In late January, the president told Congress that he intended to keep the Marines in Lebanon indefinitely. By that time, however, there was sentiment in Congress to withdraw them. The Democratic leadership of the House of Representatives was preparing a new resolution calling for their removal when the president, on February 7, 1984, ordered them to begin a phased "redeployment" (or withdrawal). In conjunction with that withdrawal, he ordered increased attacks on Syrian positions. In addition, the U.S. battleship *New Jersey* was ordered to fire on positions in the hills behind Beirut held by Syrians and by a Lebanese faction known as the Druze militia. For nine straight hours, the ship hurled one-ton shells into the hills, where they caused an enormous amount of destruction.

It is not certain just why the attacks were ordered. Different administration spokespeople gave different reasons at different times. Some indicated that they were meant to protect the Marines during their withdrawal (although they hadn't come under any attack); others that they were to help the beleaguered Lebanese government; others that they were to retaliate for enemy shelling of the Unites States ambassador's residence near Beirut.[25] The consensus of most observers, however, seems to be that they were actually ordered in frustrated retaliation for the slaughter of the sleeping Marines.

Whatever the true purpose of the shelling, the Democratic Speaker of the House of Representatives proclaimed that the congressional resolution authorizing the Marines to stay in Lebanon had "absolutely not" authorized the shelling of the Syrian and Druze positions.[26]

President Reagan used retaliation again on April 14, 1986, when he ordered eighteen American airplanes to attack Libya in response to what he claimed was Libyan President Muammar el-Qaddafi's support of widespread terrorist acts against Americans.[27]

TRUMAN'S COLD (AND HOT)
WAR AGAINST COMMUNISM

In the years since World War II, and even before, the stated reason for many of America's military actions around the world has been opposition to communism. As early as 1918, in the midst of the Russian Revolution, American military forces joined those of several other Western nations to occupy part of the Soviet Union to counter the Bolshevik efforts there.[28] Then, after the brief alliance with the Soviet Union during World War II, the enmity immediately reasserted itself. Some observers believe that even Truman's decision to drop the atomic bomb on Japan was an expression of that enmity. (The stated reason at the time was to save the thousands of American lives that would have been lost in a military invasion of Japan.) It was not, wrote the Nobel Prize-winning physicist P.M.S. Blackett, "so much the last military act of the Second World War as the first major operation of the cold diplomatic war with Russia."[29] Truman was deeply concerned with what he regarded as the communist threat. The desire to impress the Soviets with the power of America's new weapon must have been a part of his thinking.

For Truman, as for many other Americans, communism was a spreading disease. He believed that communists, led by the Soviet Union, would take over the world unless the "free world," led by the United States, checked them at every opportunity. This view of communism—and of America's role in fighting it—has provided the background for American military actions ever since. It explains why President Eisenhower sent troops to Lebanon in 1958 and why President Johnson sent troops to the Dominican Republic in 1965. And it explains why President Truman sent troops to Korea in 1950.

On June 25, 1950 (Korean time), communist North Korean forces invaded noncommunist South Korea. The following day (June 25, U.S. time), members of the United Nations Security Council met in New York. The Soviet Union was not present. The Security Council

President Harry S. Truman guided the United States into an undeclared war with North Korea.

passed a resolution condemning North Korea's action, ordering it to pull back to its own territory, and asking UN members to "render every assistance to the United Nations in the execution of this resolution."[30]

President Truman met with his advisers that evening and decided that he would send American troops to Korea. He specifically ordered those advisers *not* to mention the decision to Congress. Not until June 27 did Truman meet with congressional leaders to tell them about his decision. He then said that it had been made in compliance with the UN Security Council resolution.[31]

It isn't clear whether Truman meant the resolution mentioned above, which did not clearly authorize direct military action by UN members, or a second resolution which the Council was still in the process of debating. That second resolution asked nations to "furnish" whatever "assistance" would be "necessary . . . to repel the armed attack and to restore international peace and security. . . . "[32] In any case, by the time this second resolution was actually passed by the Security Council, U.S. troops were already fighting in Korea. The use of the UN request to justify Truman's action was interesting. Congress had certainly approved United States membership in the United Nations. But did that mean a congressional commitment to send American troops to battle whenever the United Nations asked for them? Or congressional permission for the president to do so?

Many members of Congress—most of them conservative—insisted that it did not. They argued that the Constitution took precedence over any agreement with other nations. And the Constitution made clear that only Congress could commit American troops to a large-scale foreign war.

Senator Robert Taft, the dean of American conservatives, summed up the argument best. Truman, he said, "had no authority whatever to commit American troops to Korea without consulting Congress and without Congressional approval. He could not commit our armed forces to the support of the United Nations under the terms of the UN participation act which was passed by Congress, for that act only recognized the commitment of troops in the event of a negotiation of a special military agreement with the Security Council 'which shall be subject to the approval of the Congress'. . . . The President simply usurped authority, in violation of the laws and the Constitution, when he sent troops to Korea to carry out the resolution of the UN in an undeclared war."[34]

In any case, it is clear that Truman didn't send troops to Korea because the United Nations asked him to. That request supplied a technical excuse instead of a reason. It was true that he felt that the United Nations needed support, but Truman sent troops to Korea

Seeing action in the Korean War, June 19, 1951

because he believed it was necessary to fight the spread of communism anywhere in the world. "If the Communists were permitted to force their way into the Republic of Korea without opposition from the free world," he later explained, "no small nation would ever have the courage to resist threats and aggression by stronger Communist neighbors."[35]

Besides, Truman believed, it was better to fight communism in Asia than to wait till the infection had spread to American shores. That was why Truman took another fateful action at the same time he sent troops to help the South Koreans fight communism in Korea.

He sent American money to help the French fight communism in another Asian country—a country which was then called French Indochina, but which would soon become known as Vietnam.

VIETNAM—
THE PRESIDENTS' WAR

In 1950, China, the largest and most powerful country in Asia, had just been taken over by a communist revolution led by Mao Zedong. It was widely believed in the West that China and the Soviet Union were banding together in an effort to take over the world, starting with Korea and spreading from there throughout Asia. One likely target of their efforts was the Indochinese peninsula in Southeast Asia, which included what is now called Vietnam.

Indochina had been a "protectorate" of the French until 1945. A communist—and Vietnamese nationalist—named Ho Chi Minh had assumed leadership in Vietnam in 1946. Although immensely popular with the Vietnamese, he had been quickly ousted by the French, who still had major interests in the area and had waged a guerrilla war against them ever since.

When Mao came to power in China, he offered to help Ho in his struggle against the French. Alarmed, President Truman, who was even then committing troops to fight the communists in Korea, began sending money to the French to fight the communists in Indochina, and American involvement in Vietnam began. It would continue for more than twenty years, under five presidents.[1]

AMERICAN INVOLVEMENT
IN VIETNAM

The French kept control of Indochina until 1954. That May, the French outpost at Dien Bien Phu fell to the rebels after a long siege. The French and the Indochinese negotiated a peace settlement at Geneva, in which Indochina was divided into three nations: Laos, Cambodia, and Vietnam. Vietnam, however, was split in two, into a communist North Vietnam, led by Ho, and a noncommunist South Vietnam, led by Premier Ngo Dinh Diem. This division was intended to be temporary. The Geneva agreement called for nationwide elections, which would unify North and South Vietnam under a single national government, to be held two years later.

By this time, the Korean War was over and there was a new administration in the United States, headed by President Dwight D. Eisenhower. The Eisenhower administration was determined to block any further communist gains in Southeast Asia. To help accomplish this, it formed the Southeast Asia Treaty Organization (SEATO). SEATO's members—the United States, Australia, France, Great Britain, New Zealand, Pakistan, the Philippines, and Thailand—all pledged to consult one another on ways to protect the "security" of Southeast Asia. The treaty establishing SEATO was ratified in the usual way by the United States Senate.

Early in 1955, United States involvement in Vietnam was intensified when it took over the training of the South Vietnamese Army. The Eisenhower administration had over three hundred American military "advisers" in Vietnam by that time. Although the United States had not been directly involved in the negotiations in Geneva, the treaty allowed up to 685 such advisers, and the administration needed no specific congressional authorization to have them there, since they were there only to train Vietnamese for combat.

In fact, there was no ongoing combat between the government and communist forces in Vietnam at that time at all, only clashes between groups feuding for control of the South Vietnamese government. The American advisers were seen partly as a sign of American support for the Diem government in its struggles with its political rivals.

When the time came for the agreed-upon elections, the Diem government refused to allow them to take place. The United States supported the cancellation of the elections,[2] because, as Eisenhower later acknowledged, Ho Chi Minh would certainly have won them.[3]

By 1957, the guerrilla war had been resumed, this time not against the French but against the Diem government. Communist South Vietnamese, with support from the north, were battling to bring down the Diem government. American advisers were continuing to train the government forces, but it wasn't until July 8, 1959, that the first of these advisers was killed. The next year, the number of American advisers climbed well over the limit placed by the Geneva treaty.

In 1961, the year President John F. Kennedy took office, the president raised the number of American military forces in Vietnam even higher, to 3,200.

Meanwhile, Diem's government was rapidly losing what little popularity it had ever had, both in Vietnam and in the United States. It was acknowledged to be both corrupt and oppressive, and the American government was finding it increasingly hard to justify support of it. Finally, in November of 1963, the U.S. government allowed a group of Vietnamese army officers to overthrow Diem and execute him.

The next year and a half was a time of chaos in South Vietnam, as thirteen different governments tried to rule the country while the guerrilla war intensified. In the United States, President Kennedy was assassinated, and his vice president, Lyndon Johnson, took over the presidency. The number of American advisers continued to climb until it reached nearly twenty thousand, but they were still said to be there in a training rather than combat role.[4]

THE INCIDENT IN
THE TONKIN GULF

On August 2, 1964, three North Vietnamese torpedo boats were sighted bearing down on the U.S. destroyer *Maddox* in the Gulf of Tonkin, off the coast of North Vietnam. After firing three warning shots across their bows, the *Maddox* fired on the boats themselves. Two of the torpedo boats fired one torpedo each at the U.S. ship and then fled. The other continued to close on the *Maddox*, which opened fire on her. Later, the boat was reported to have been hit, and it presumably sank. In any event, it did no damage to the American ship. Meanwhile, American planes from an aircraft carrier in the South China Sea located and fired on the escaping torpedo boats.[5]

Two days later, the *Maddox* and another American ship, the *Turner Joy*, were reportedly attacked by several North Vietnamese gunboats. After what was described as a three-and-one-half-hour battle, two of the gunboats were sunk and the rest escaped.

That night, President Johnson appeared on American television. He was solemn. "It is my duty to the American people," he said, "to report that renewed hostile actions against United States ships on the high seas in the Gulf of Tonkin have today required me to order the military forces of the United States to take action in reply."

"We Americans know," the president continued, "though others seem to forget—the risk of spreading conflict. We still seek no wider war. . . . But it is my con-

President Lyndon B. Johnson signs the 1964
Tonkin Gulf Resolution, which he hailed as
a new example of democracy's "capacity to
act decisively and swiftly against aggression."
Unfortunately, the decisive and swift action
that followed didn't win the Vietnam War
or save the lives of the over fifty thousand
Americans who died in it.

sidered conviction that firmness in the right is indispensable."[6]

Over the next several hours, American jets and propeller-driven A-1 Skyraiders struck at several sites on the North Vietnamese coast, destroying (it was reported) half the patrol boats in the North Vietnamese Navy and several large oil tanks.

Before addressing the nation on television, Johnson had called several congressional leaders to the White House and told them of the impending attacks on North Vietnam. As reported by *Time*, Johnson made it clear that he was "informing" them, "not asking their advice. 'These are our plans,' he snapped." No objections were raised.[7]

In that same meeting, he asked the leaders to give him a congressional resolution supporting what he'd already done and authorizing him to take further actions if necessary. He would get that resolution from Congress within days; and it would prove to be the major turning point in the American involvement in the Vietnam War.

THE TONKIN GULF RESOLUTION

On August 5, 1964, the day after his national television appearance, the president sent a message to Congress formally asking for the resolution he had asked the congressional leaders to give him the night before. In that message, he repeated the assurance he had made on television: "the United States intends no rashness and seeks no wider war."[8]

Congress was in a mood to give the president any resolution he asked for. American ships, presumably sailing peaceably in neutral waters, had been attacked. Congress, no less than the public (maybe more than the public) was outraged. One indication of that outrage was the ease with which the resolution swept through Congress. The Senate passed it overwhelmingly, on a vote of 88 to 2, after only nine hours of debate. The only two nay votes were cast by two Democratic senators, Ernest Gruening of Alaska and Wayne Morse of Oregon, both opponents of American involvement in Vietnam. The House passed it 416 to 0, after less than an hour of debate.[9]

That resolution would become the center of the controversy over presidential versus congressional war powers in the Vietnam era. In its most quoted passage at that time, the resolution referred back to the Commander-in-Chief clause of the Constitution. "Congress approves and supports the determination of the President, as Commander in Chief, to take all necessary measures to repel any armed attack against the forces of the United States and to prevent further aggression." That passage seemed to refer to situations like the one in the Tonkin Gulf, in which American forces were attacked. But in another passage, less noticed at the time, the resolution used language that suggested it might have a broader significance.

"The United States regards as vital to its national interest and to world peace the maintenance of international peace and security in Southeast Asia. Consonant with the Constitution and the Charter of the United Nations and in accordance with its obligations under the Southeast Asia Collective Defense Treaty, the United States is, therefore, prepared, as the President determines, to take all necessary steps, including the use of armed force, to assist any member or protocol state of the Southeast Asia Collective Defense Treaty requesting assistance in defense of its freedom."[10]

President Johnson, as well as his successor, Richard Nixon, escalated American involvement in Vietnam enormously over the next five years. That escalation took place almost entirely by presidential order, without any further specific act of Congress that either declared a war or directly gave the president authority to conduct one. Many of the presidents' defenders, both inside of Congress and out, used the Tonkin Gulf Resolution to justify their actions. They didn't need any further authorization from Congress, defenders argued. They'd already been given all the authority they needed in the Tonkin Gulf Resolution. Congress had already proclaimed the country prepared, *"as the President determines,* to take *all* necessary steps, *including the use of armed force. . . ."* [Italics mine.] That, defenders claimed, was as good as a declaration of war would have been.

In a sense, Wayne Morse, the Senate's most spirited opponent of American involvement in Vietnam, had admitted as much himself—in advance—when he explained why he was voting againt the resolution. He would not, he said, support what amounted to "a predated declaration of war."[11]

Johnson administration officials, including Johnson himself, argued that the president didn't actually *need* the resolution to do what he did. He had the inherent power even without it.[12] Later on, Senator Robert Dole would make a similar claim for the Nixon administration in a Senate debate over repeal of the resolution. "(Administration officials) are not relying on the Gulf of Tonkin Resolution," he said. "They have not relied on the Gulf of Tonkin Resolution."[13] That was, of course, implying an even broader claim for presidential power. Those presidential defenders who relied on the resolution were at least acknowledging that Congress had a necessary role in authorizing when, where, and how American military forces were to be used. But those who claimed that the president had the power to carry on an action such as the war in Vietnam without such congressional authorization were implying a lesser role for Congress. And maybe no role at all. In any case, it's certainly true that when the resolution was finally repealed, American military actions in Vietnam continued. (See below.)

Still, in the years that followed its passage, the resolution served as a kind of buffer to any criticism of presidential actions in regard to Vietnam. It seemed to make the question of the presidents' power to act on their own irrelevant. Congress, it was argued again and again, had already spoken, and had given the president the go-ahead.

Opponents of the war argued that the resolution had never been intended as a go-ahead for a wider war. Hadn't President Johnson repeated, over and over again, that the United States wanted "no wider war"? Hadn't he even used the phrase in his message to Congress asking for the resolution? Representatives and senators had gone out of their way during the brief debates leading to passage of the resolution to make clear that they were *not* voting for a declaration of war. As Congressman Dante Fascell put it: "This resolution is not a declaration of war. The language of the resolution makes that clear as does the legislative history. . . . Furthermore, no one here today has advocated a declaration of war."[14]

Even more importantly, opponents of the war claimed, whatever the purpose of the resolution had been, it was obtained by fraud. The administration had won it from Congress by deception, by appealing to their emotions in the wake of the attack on American ships in the Tonkin Gulf. But that attack—if there had ever been such an attack—had been seriously misrepresented by the administration. No damage had been done to American ships at all, in either attack. The only American casualties had come not during the attacks themselves, but in the retaliations for the attacks launched by the U.S. military. Even with the benefit of every doubt, opponents claimed, the resolution had been an emotional overreaction to what had been a very minor incident. As such, it should not have been used to justify an extended and terrible war.

Some opponents, like Senator George S. McGovern, argued that more than simple misrepresentation was involved. They claimed that there had been deliberate deception on the part of the administration, and that "Congress was a primary target of the pattern of deception practiced by the Executive department."[15] Congress was told that U.S. ships had not been involved in military operations in the Gulf of Tonkin in the days before the attacks, while later evidence showed that they were. The resolution itself, supposedly a reaction to the attacks, had not been written in response to them at all. In fact, its key language had been drawn up by Assistant Secretary of State William Bundy two months *before* the events in the Gulf. The administration had been looking for—and, in fact, trying to provoke—some action on the part of the North Vietnamese that would make it possible to sell the resolution to Congress. When the incident in the Gulf came along, it gave them that opportunity.

Or did it? Some critics, including Senator William Fulbright, at that time the chairman of the Senate Foreign Relations Committee, have suggested that the incident may not have 'come along' at all. Fulbright, who had been instrumental in passing the resolution in the first place, later felt bitterly deceived. In 1968, he held Senate hearings questioning whether there had ever been any attack on American ships at all, or whether the Johnson administration had simply manufactured the supposed attack to gain congressional support for escalating American involvement in the war.[16]

If that were the case, the deception succeeded. In the five years that followed the Tonkin Gulf Resolution, Congress consistently went along with whatever Presidents Johnson and Nixon wanted to do in Southeast Asia. And what they wanted to do, it seemed, was to escalate the U.S. involvement in the war. That escalation was dramatic, and sustained over a long period of time.

Marine combat troops landed in Vietnam for the first time in March 1965. Within months, the administration announced (after the fact) that U.S. forces had been authorized to take part in actual combat there. By October, 148,000 American military personnel were in the country. By the end of 1966, the number had more than doubled to 389,000, and by the middle of 1967, it had climbed to 463,000. By that time, too, American forces had entered the so-called Demilitarized Zone, in order to interfere with North Vietnamese access to the south. By mid-1969, the number of U.S. forces in Vietnam had jumped again, to over half a million men and women.[17] And, in all that time, according to Senator George McGovern, "Congress was never consulted . . . about any significant steps in the escalation."[18]

In a sense, there was no practical reason to consult Congress. In the eyes of presidential supporters, Congress had willingly given its agreement in advance, in the Tonkin Gulf Resolution. In the eyes of presidential critics, the resolution had amounted to a kind of surrender to the president on the part of Congress. In the words of the Congressional Report on National Commitments, issued in 1967: "The Gulf of Tonkin Resolution represents the extreme point in the process of congressional erosion."[19]

Although it may not have been consulted, Congress regularly provided the money for the escalation. Its willingness to do so may have come partly from the fact that American armed forces were in combat. Even those members of Congress who had doubts about the war felt unable to cut off support for them. In this respect, the more U.S. involvement there was, the harder it became to oppose it. (As a congressman, Abraham Lincoln had felt the same pressure at the time of the Mexican War.)

The extent of congressional acquiescence in the war is shown by Defense Department estimates of funds spent for U.S. activities in Southeast Asia during those years. In the year following the Tonkin Gulf Resolution, appropriations jumped from $100 million the year before to $5.8 billion. The next year, they soared to $20.1 billion. By fiscal year 1969, they reached their peak of $28.8 billion.[20]

By that time, despite the rising appropriations, feeling about the war had begun to turn around, both in Congress and among the general public. Already by 1968, sentiment had turned so far against the war within President Johnson's own party that he withdrew as a candidate for renomination for president. His vice president, Hubert Humphrey, eventually won the nomination but lost the election. The Republican victor, Richard Nixon, had campaigned saying that he had a plan to end the war, although he never explained what that plan was.

Once in office, Nixon made an effort to "Vietnamize" the war, cutting back on the number of American ground troops there. However, he also expanded the war by secretly bombing Vietnam's neutral neighbor, Cambodia. Eventually, an ex-Air Force officer would testify before a congressional committee that the records of at least 3,500 bombing raids had been falsified in 1969 and 1970 to hide the fact that Cambodia was being bombed.[21] To hide it from the American public and from Congress, that is. The Cambodians obviously already knew they were being bombed.

On June 25, 1969, the Senate tried to reassert congressional prerogatives, by passing (70 to 16) the so-called National Commitments Resolution. The resolution expressed "the sense of the Senate that a national

During the 1968 presidential race, Richard M. Nixon claimed to have a secret plan to end the Vietnam War.

President Nixon expanded the Vietnam War by invading Cambodia before eventually ending U.S. military involvement in 1972.

commitment by the United States results only from affirmative action taken by the executive and legislative branches of the United States Government by means of a treaty, statute, or concurrent resolution of both Houses of Congress specifically providing for such commitment."[22]

That same year, fearing a presidential expansion of the war into other nations, Congress passed the Cooper–Church Amendment, which forbade the administration to use any funds to introduce "American ground combat troops" into Vietnam's neighbors, Laos and Thailand.[23] But the Congress, which had never been informed of the secret bombing, had missed the intended target. In April 1970, President Nixon ordered an "incursion" (or invasion) into another of Vietnam's neighbors—Cambodia—instead. In answer to those who charged that this invasion of a neutral country was against both American and international law, Nixon responded indirectly. "We will not be humiliated," he said. "We will not be defeated."[24]

In 1971, first the Senate and then the House voted to repeal the Tonkin Gulf Resolution. The Nixon administration, knowing it would lose anyway, didn't fight the repeal effort. It claimed that it didn't need the resolution to carry on its efforts in Vietnam in any case. President Nixon signed the repeal into law on January 12, 1971. The next month, disregarding not only the repeal but the Cooper–Church Amendment as well, Nixon ordered U.S. combat troops across the Vietnamese border into Laos. But the U.S. involvement in Vietnam was coming to an end. The U.S. troops' combat role in Southeast Asia finally ended on June 17, 1972.

The war in Vietnam had been the longest in American history, and one of the bloodiest. It had been carried out almost exclusively by presidential order. Not only had it not been declared, it had never been directly authorized by either house of Congress. It was truly the ultimate presidents' war.

CHECKING PRESIDENTIAL POWER

What can be done when presidents overstep their legitimate war powers—or when Congress or the people think that they do?

The Constitution gives Congress two clear options: the power of the purse and the power of impeachment. These would seem to be more than enough. If Congress decides the president is going too far, it can cut off the funds he needs to pursue the action. If the action is already over, or is so offensive to Congress that stronger steps seem necessary, it can impeach the president, convict him of overstepping his powers, and throw him out of office.

In practice, these congressional powers have proven surprisingly ineffective. The president can order immediate military action; once this has been done, Congress is powerless to undo it. As we have seen, it is extraordinarily difficult for Congress to refuse funds for an action already under way. Once U.S. forces are involved in actual fighting, there is a natural reluctance to back down in the face of an enemy. For Congress to cut off funds would be a kind of surrender, and most politicians find voting for an American surrender both politically and psychologically painful.

There's an even greater reluctance to desert forces in the field. Many senators and representatives who opposed the U.S. involvement in Vietnam continued to vote for funds to support it, because they could not refuse funds to support American soldiers in combat situations. Despite his own strong opposition to the Mexican War, a century earlier, Congressman Abraham Lincoln voted for funds to pay for it for this reason.

For most politicians it is as painful to impeach a president as to cut off military funds in wartime. Whatever the framers of the Constitution intended, the office and person of the president has assumed an enormous significance. In ancient times, one of the most horrible crimes of all was rebellion against the king. It smacked of overturning the society and destroying the state. Although the American president is not a king, the thought of impeaching a president arouses something of the same fear and distress in American society. The extent of this fear is suggested by the fact that in the over two centuries of the country's existence, *no* president has been formally turned out of office by the impeachment process. Only two have even come close. One, Richard Nixon, resigned before the process could be completed. The other, Andrew Johnson, was acquitted in his trial before the Senate.

While the powers of the purse and impeachment are the two most direct powers granted to Congress in these matters, they are not the only ones. Congress— and the people—have other recourses against a chief executive whom they believe to be overstepping his powers.

A CHALLENGE IN THE COURTS

One other recourse is an appeal to the third branch of government, the courts. War powers claimed by the president have often been challenged in the courts.

Most of the cases have involved specific actions—for example, the taking over of a steel company during time of war. Sometimes the president has been upheld in such cases, sometimes not.

When it comes to matters directly involving foreign policy, however, the courts have been extremely reluctant to limit presidential authority. In the case of *United States* v. *Curtiss-Wright*, the Supreme Court ruled that where foreign policy was concerned, the president was to be granted a "degree of discretion and freedom from statutory restriction which would not be admissible were domestic affairs alone involved." This was because the president has the best "opportunity of knowing the conditions which prevail in foreign countries." The Court went on to note, "especially is this true in time of war."[1]

During the Vietnam War, a number of draft resisters challenged the constitutionality of the president's power to send troops into combat. Supported by the American Civil Liberties Union (ACLU), they argued that the government had no right to force them to serve in a war that was unconstitutional because it had not been declared by Congress.

The courts were reluctant to hear these cases. They ducked many of them with technical reasons, or by ruling that the Vietnam issue was a "political question" and therefore not "justiciable." That is, that it was outside the authority of the courts to decide.[2] Other challenges were dismissed for reasons of standing. The courts ruled, for example, that receiving a draft notice didn't entitle a person to question the constitutionality of the war, because he (women were not being drafted) might never be sent to Vietnam.

In one case, involving soldiers who had actually received orders to be shipped to Vietnam, a court ruled against them, not on the grounds that *they* lacked standing, but that the court did. "The fundamental division of authority and power established by the Constitution precludes judges from overseeing the conduct of foreign policy on the use and disposition of military power; these matters are plainly the exclusive provinces of Congress and the Executive."[3] The Supreme Court refused to hear an appeal of the case, so the lower court ruling was allowed to stand.

Two other important cases (*Berk* v. *Laird* and *Orlando* v. *Laird*) resulted in defeats for the two members of the armed forces who had brought the suits. (Secretary of Defense Melvin Laird was technically the defendant in both cases.) The court didn't rule that the president had a right to conduct a war without congressional approval, however. Instead, it held that Congress had in effect *given* that approval.

"The Congress and the Executive have taken mutual and joint action in the prosecution and support of military operations in Southeast Asia from the beginning of these operations," the appeals court ruled. Congress had consistently voted money to pay for the war. What's more, it had given specific authorization for it in the Tonkin Gulf Resolution. Although that resolution "was occasioned by specific naval incidents in the Gulf of Tonkin, [it] was expressed in broad language which clearly showed the state of mind of the Congress and its intention fully to implement and support the military and naval actions taken by and planned to be taken by the President at that time in Southeast Asia, and as might be required in the future 'to prevent further aggression.' "[4] Ironically, then, the resolution—which both the Johnson and Nixon administrations had claimed not to need—was a key factor in the court decision which upheld the legitimacy of their conduct of the war in Vietnam.

The decision in the *Berk* and *Orlando* cases was considered important by both sides in the war powers controversy. The supporters of presidential power hailed it as proof of the constitutionality of the Vietnam War. Opponents, meanwhile, hailed it for establishing "the principle of judicial review of Executive warmaking" and claimed that it had "utterly destroyed" the "myth of inherent presidential authority to wage war."[5]

THE WAR POWERS RESOLUTION

Seemingly more significant, at least at the time, was a major effort in Congress to check the president's power to commit American troops to war. After three years of hearings and debates, that effort resulted in a joint resolution of both the House and the Senate, known as the War Powers Resolution of 1973.

The resolution's stated purpose was to "fulfill the intent of the framers of the Constitution of the United States and insure that the collective judgement of both the Congress and the President will apply to the introduction of United States Armed Forces into hostilities, or into situations where imminent involvement in hostilities is clearly indicated by the circumstances, and to the continued use of such forces in hostilities or in such situations."[6]

To that end, the resolution contained several specific provisions. They required that "in every possible instance" the president should consult with Congress before introducing U.S. armed forces into "such situations," unless Congress had already declared war or specifically authorized the president to act. Where consultation in advance was impossible, the president was required to inform Congress of his actions within forty-eight hours of taking them. Then, if Congress didn't make a declaration of war or other authorization within sixty to ninety days (depending on circumstances) the president would have to call off the action involved. Should Congress not want to wait for the ninety days, it could order a halt to the action itself by passing a joint resolution, which would not be subject to a presidential veto.

The War Powers Resolution was originally passed on October 24, 1973, but was vetoed by President Nixon on the grounds that it was unconstitutional. Congress then passed it again, with the two-thirds majority needed to override the veto. The vote was 75 to 18 in the Senate and 284 to 135 in the House. The key votes in the House were provided by six liberal Democrats, who had voted against the bill the first time around not because they thought it limited the president too much but because they thought it limited him too little. They argued that by allowing the president to introduce troops into any foreign hostilities at all without consulting Congress, it granted him authority that was not constitutionally his. In the end, however, they voted with the majority to override Nixon's veto, and the War Powers Resolution became law.[7]

IS THE WAR POWERS
ACT EFFECTIVE?

Virtually no one seems satisfied with the way the War Powers Act has worked in practice. Every president since Nixon has argued that it is unconstitutional and that it interferes with their ability to conduct foreign policy.[8] Congressional supporters of the act protest that presidents ignore it whenever it suits them or find ways to work around it and render it ineffective.

The Supreme Court has not ruled directly on the constitutionality of the act. It did, however, make a ruling that casts some doubt on the constitutionality of one provision of the law. As the act is written, the president cannot veto congressional actions taken under it. In a case involving an entirely different law, the Court struck down a similar veto-proof provision. As always, though, the Court seems reluctant to step between Congress and the president when it comes to the war powers. As the one-time chief of staff of the Senate Foreign Relations Committee, Pat M. Holt, has written, "Both supporters and opponents of the resolution . . . have expressed doubts that the Supreme Court will ever rule on the issue."[9]

One obvious problem with the act is the vagueness of its terms. What does "consultation" with "Congress" mean? Neither term is defined. Exactly who in Congress is to be consulted? The Senate, which the Constitution gives particular powers in foreign affairs? The House? Both bodies? The entire memberships of both? The members of the key committees handling military affairs? The majority and minority leaders of each House? The act itself gives no clue.

In practice, presidents have usually only submitted written reports of military actions well after the actions have already taken place. When given at all, prior notice has usually been limited to a handful of congressional leaders. (This was true, for example, of the raid on Libya.)

However, congressional protests over presidential noncompliance with the act have not centered on the issue of *who* should be informed. Instead, they have centered on the lateness of reports submitted under the act, or else the lack of them—and the lack of any real consultation.

What is consultation? Does it mean the simple process of informing Congress, or something more? A congressional report on the War Powers Resolution argued that it meant much more: "Consultation in this provision means that a decision is pending on a problem and that Members of Congress are being asked by the President for their advice and opinions and, in appropriate circumstances, their approval of action contemplated."[10]

In that sense, there has been little if any consulta-

President Reagan sent U.S. troops to trouble spots around the world without declaring war. Like other presidents before him, he was sometimes intensely criticized for his actions.

tion in recent years. President Ford, for example, reported that he had informed Congress of the attempted rescue of the captured ship and crew of the U.S.S. *Mayaguez*, in the waters off Cambodia, only *after* the order had already been given. His successor, President Carter, failed to notify Congress that he was sending troops to rescue American hostages held captive in Iran in 1980.[11] Each president apparently decided that the missions needed secrecy if they were to have a chance to succeed, and that they therefore were not among the "every possible instance(s)" which required them to consult with Congress in advance.

President Reagan's first report to Congress on the 1983 invasion of Grenada came on October 25, when American forces were already fighting and dying on the small Caribbean island. Although Reagan did report under the War Powers Act, he specifically refrained from citing the section of the act that would have formally activated the sixty- to ninety-day time limit on unauthorized actions. Congressional leaders argued the limit had been automatically activated anyway, but the question became moot (or irrelevant) when the combat troops were removed well before sixty days were up.[12]

When he had sent Marines into Lebanon in 1982, Reagan had again reported to Congress but specifically avoided citing the section of the act that would have required congressional approval to allow them to stay there longer than 90 days. It was at least arguable, at first, since the Marines were there as part of a multinational peacekeeping force, that they were not engaged "in hostilities" or in a situation "where imminent involvement in hostilities" was "clearly indicated by the circumstances." In that case, the time limit provision did not apply. Even when the Marines began coming under attacks of various kinds, the president still refused to acknowledge the applicability of the "hostilities" provision. Sentiment rose in Congress to invoke the War Powers Act, and several different bills were introduced to do so.

A compromise was reached between Congress and the president. A resolution was passed on September 29, 1983, invoking the War Powers Act and making the continued presence of the Marines in Lebanon subject to congressional approval. But in the same resolution, Congress approved their presence there for another eighteen months.

President Reagan signed the compromise on October 13, 1983. In doing so, he technically accepted the principle of the War Powers Act. Even so, he continued to quarrel with the notion that the Marines were involved in "hostilities." "I would note," he argued, "that the initiation of isolated or infrequent acts of violence against United States armed forces does not necessarily constitute actual or imminent involvement in

"Trust me.
I promise you
I won't get in
over my head."

hostilities, even if casualties to those forces result."[13] Ten days later, on October 23, 1983, the truck bomb exploded in Beirut, killing 241 Marines.

There has been some sentiment in Congress for invoking the War Powers Act in regard to the presence of U.S. military personnel in Central America. The Reagan administration has accused the Sandinista government of Nicaragua of undermining its neighbors, including El Salvador and Honduras. To counter it, the United States has, for a number of years, assisted the other governments of Central America in many ways— including covert, or secret, actions by the CIA and others to support anti-Sandinista revolutionaries, known as *contras*, inside Nicaragua and in Honduras. Such actions are generally acknowledged to be beyond the scope of the War Powers Act.

There have been American militiary advisers in El Salvador for several years, and large numbers of U.S. troops—sometimes several thousand—have been moved into and out of Honduras. The Reagan administration has argued that none of these military personnel is there to engage in combat. According to the State Department, the advisers in El Salvador are there to train, not to fight. They "will not act as combat advisors, and will not accompany Salvadoran forces in combat . . . or in any . . . situation where combat is likely."[14] The many troops in Honduras, meanwhile, are there primarily to conduct training exercises. Because of their noncombat roles, the Reagan administration has argued, these forces do not activate the War Powers Act.

Many members of Congress remain unconvinced. They suspect that the troops in Honduras, near the Nicaraguan border, were sent to be ready for a possible invasion. Even if this is not the case, they worry that the troops will provoke actions from the Nicaraguans that could embroil the United States in a war in Central America before Congress had a chance to act on the issue. Still, while there have been efforts on the part of some members of Congress to invoke the War Powers Act, Congress has not done so.

In the summer of 1987, the Reagan administration announced plans to offer U.S. protection to Kuwaiti oil tankers in the Persian Gulf. The ships would even be allowed to sail under the U.S. flag. Some members of Congress felt that the proposed action should be formally reported under the War Powers Act, since it seemed likely that the reflagging would result in the American forces being engaged in combat. (An American ship, the *Stark*, had already come under attack by an Iraqi plane in the Gulf, with the loss of thirty-seven American lives.) Administration officials argued that there was no need to invoke the act, however. They had no reason, they said, to believe that the reflagging of the Kuwaiti vessels would result in "imminent hostilities," or danger to American forces.

The first ship escorted by American vessels was

In 1987, President Reagan ordered the U.S. Navy to escort Kuwaiti tankers— flying the American flag—in the Persian Gulf. Many people, but not the president, believed the War Powers Act should have been invoked.

damaged by a mine. The following weeks saw several small incidents between U.S. forces and Iranian ships and planes in the Gulf. Early in October, an American helicopter was fired on by several Iranian gunboats.[15] American forces captured the gunboats and discovered equipment for advanced Stinger land-to-air missiles on board. As a result, American forces were reportedly ordered to prepare to fire on Iranian ships and planes at the slightest sign of possible hostile action.[16]

In light of all this, a number of senators, led by Low-ell P. Weicker of Connecticut, insisted that the president should report to Congress and trigger the act. The administration, however, refused to do so. Some administration officials even appeared on television to suggest that Iran was deliberately taking hostile action in order to provoke Congress into limiting the president by invoking the War Powers Act. The implication was that any member of Congress who (like Weicker) favored imposing the act was playing into the hands of the hostile Iranians.

The Senate eventually reached a compromise on October 21, 1987. It called for the president to report to Congress on his policy in the Gulf within thirty days. The Congress would then have thirty more days in which to approve or disapprove of that policy.[17] Few members of Congress were really happy with the compromise. Even so, the Senate majority leader, Robert Byrd, refused to declare that the War Powers Act was dead. He did, however, acknowledge that it was "in intensive care."[18]

COVERT ACTIONS AND CONGRESSIONAL OVERSIGHT

One of the most common of all reasons given for allowing the president to act without consulting Congress is the need for secrecy. It is often necessary, proponents of presidential authority claim, for the United States to act covertly (in secret). This is true in many branches of espionage, in rescue operations, in helping the opponents of repressive governments around the world, and sometimes in undertaking actual military operations against our enemies. Such things, they argue, cannot be done publicly, and if they are to be done in secret they must be sometimes done by the executive branch alone, without informing Congress until they are over. The reason, as Walter Berns, adjunct scholar at the American Enterprise Institute, once put it, is that secrecy is a "capacity that cannot be found in the Congress of the United States."[19]

Opponents of presidential power argue that presidents often misuse the supposed need for secrecy. Besides, they argue, it is simply not true that Congress cannot keep a secret. Congressman Barney Frank of Massachusetts said that there has never been a leak of important information as a result of consultation with Congress on a matter of national security.[20]

Frank has also pointed out that presidents have two different reasons for keeping actions secret. One is because secrecy is necessary to carry out a particular action. The second is because if the action were made public, Congress (and the people) would oppose it. The first reason, Frank says, is legitimate; the second is not. And all too often, opponents argue, it is the second reason that produces the so-called "need" for secrecy. They point to the revelations of 1986–1987, commonly known as Iranscam, as a prime example of the abuse of the "need" for secrecy.

In late 1986, a Middle-East newspaper revealed that the Reagan administration had secretly sold arms to the government of Iran. It was the same Iranian government that had held American hostages, laid mines in the Persian Gulf, and was suspected of being behind the bombing of the Marine barracks in Lebanon. Such sales were against publicly declared American foreign policy, and took place while the Reagan administration itself was pressuring America's allies *not* to sell arms to Iran. What, critics ask, was the national security need for that secrecy?

The Iranians knew they were buying the weapons. Only Congress, the American people, and America's allies were kept in the dark. In Iranscam, as in other cases, critics claim, actions were kept secret not because those actions would be in danger if America's *enemies* found out about them, but because they might be in danger if the American *people* found out about them. And if the American people would oppose a mili-

IN THE DARK IN THE WHITE HOUSE

President Reagan and his advisers secretly tried to combine getting hostages out of Lebanon by selling weapons to Iran, with helping the contras in Nicaragua. Although Iranscam/ Contragate was not a military operation, both Poindexter (right) and North held high ranks in the armed forces.

tary action, the opponents argue, the president has no right to carry out that action in their name, secretly or otherwise.

OVERSIGHT

Starting in the 1970s, there have been several congressional efforts to gain some kind of check on the president's power to conduct covert operations. The most important of these have focused on the idea of oversight, the right of the Congress to be aware of executive actions and to consult and advise in connection with them.

The Congressional Oversight Act of 1980 ordered the president to report any significant covert activities to the House and Senate Intelligence Committees; such notification was to come, whenever possible, *before* the activities were carried out. In those extraordinary circumstances in which prior notification was impossible, it should come in a "timely" fashion. The act did not give the committees the right to veto the covert action, but it did give them the right to comment on it, and to inform other relevant committees of the action if they considered it necessary.

In the years since 1980, the question of what is and what is not "timely" notice has caused friction between the president and Congress. Congress has tended to interpret "timely" as meaning "prompt," whereas critics have charged that the president has interpreted it to mean—essentially—"never."[21] In the case of the arms sales to Iran, for example, the president didn't inform Congress until after a news story from the Middle East had already revealed the sales, more than a year after they had begun. Once the sales themselves were made public, it was revealed that some of the money received from Iran had been diverted to help the Nicaraguan *contras.*

In the wake of the resulting scandal, the Reagan administration made a concession to Congress. It agreed to inform Congress within forty-eight hours of any future covert actions—except in what the White House called the "most exceptional circumstances."[22] Given the administration's record, however, several members of Congress expressed doubt whether the White House could be relied on to keep its agreement.

THE FINGER ON THE BUTTON

The question of the war powers has been a major issue from the beginning of the United States of America. It was hotly debated at the Federal Convention in 1787, and it is still being hotly debated in Congress today, more than 200 years later. If anything, the debate is hotter now—more urgent—than it has ever been before. The reason is the special urgency brought about by the existence of nuclear weapons.

Nuclear weapons are, of course, enormously powerful. There is no question that they can destroy cities, and even whole countries, in moments. Some scientists argue that through a process called nuclear winter, a large-scale nuclear war could actually destroy all life on the planet.

The power in the hands of any nation or individual with control over a large number of such nuclear weapons is frightening. It is the power to bring about the certain deaths of millions of people, and the potential death of everyone on Earth. The United States has that power. It is the possessor of one of the two largest arsenals of nuclear weapons ever assembled. And the power to use those weapons is in the hands of one person: the president. It always has been.

The atomic bomb—the ancestor of today's more sophisticated and vastly more powerful weapons—was developed secretly in the United States during World War II. The power to use it, or not to use it, rested from the first in the hands of the president of the United States. In August 1945, President Harry S. Truman made the single most fateful decision ever made by the leader of a nation at war. He decided to use the atomic bomb. On August 6, the bomb was dropped on Hiroshima, Japan, instantly killing or maiming some 150,000 Japanese civilians and assuring thousands more of eventual disease and death. Three days later, again on the orders of the president, an even larger bomb was dropped on the city of Nagasaki.[1]

The fear of atomic—and now nuclear—war has hung over the world ever since. Only a few people in history have ever had the power to make that fear come true. Some have been the leaders of the Soviet Union and of the few other countries that possess nuclear weapons and the means of delivering them. The others have been presidents of the United States.

The procedures those other countries may have for determining whether to start—or to deliberately risk—a nuclear war are beyond the concern of this book. But what about the United States? How are those decisions made here? The answer seems to be that they are made by the president of the United States. He may take the advice of whatever advisers he may choose to consult, but the ultimate power rests with him, and with him alone. That was certainly the case when Truman made his decision in the summer of 1945. And it was the case again in October 1962, when, many people believe, the world came the closest it has ever come to an actual nuclear confrontation.

President John F. Kennedy almost led the U.S. into nuclear war with the Soviet Union in 1962—without any action by Congress.

That fall, President Kennedy and his advisers learned that the Soviet Union had put missiles—capable of delivering nuclear warheads anywhere in North America—on the island of Cuba, some ninety miles off Florida. Without consulting Congress, Kennedy considered a number of possible responses, including an air strike against the missile bases in Cuba and even an out-and-out invasion of that country. He finally decided to demand that the missile sites be destroyed and the Soviet weapons removed from Cuba. In the meantime, the United States would "quarantine" Cuba, preventing, by military force if necessary, any further weapons from being delivered to Cuba. (The action was to be called a "quarantine," rather than a blockade, because a blockade could be considered an act of war.)

In effect, Kennedy was daring the Soviet Union to try and break through the "quarantine." There was no question in Kennedy's mind that his action could result in nuclear war with the Soviets. In a televised speech on October 22 he made what amounted to both a promise and a threat: "We will not prematurely or unnecessarily risk the costs of world-wide nuclear war in which even the fruits of victory would be ashes in our mouth, but neither will we shrink from that risk at any time it must be faced."[2] Kennedy was taking that risk without specific authorization from Congress and without asking for any. Not only did Kennedy fail to inform Congress of his decision in advance, he specifically concealed it from them. It wasn't until two hours before he went on television to announce his decision to the world that he finally met with twenty congressional leaders to tell them what was happening. That meeting was later referred to by Kennedy adviser Theodore Sorensen as "the only sour note of the day." Interestingly, some of the congressional leaders pushed for even stronger action than Kennedy was already taking. But Kennedy rejected both their advice and the suggestion that he needed congressional approval for what he was doing. He was acting, in Sorensen's words, "by Executive Order, presidential proclamation and inherent powers," not under any authority granted by Congress.[3]

Proponents of presidential power might argue that only the president can make the decision whether or not to use nuclear weapons—or, like Kennedy, to start out on a course that might lead to their use. In a world in which missiles can travel from one country to another in a few minutes, the idea of consulting with Congress over their use is obsolete.

Others would point out that the authority to respond to an attack is quite different than the authority to use nuclear weapons—or to threaten their use—without being attacked first. (It should be remembered that as far back as the Constitutional Convention, a distinction was made between the power "to repel sudden attacks" and the power to begin a war.) They might argue that the awesome power of nuclear weapons makes it more important than ever that the power to commit America to war be kept out of the hands of any single individual, even the president of the United States.

Still others would argue that the whole idea of committing the United States—and inevitably the world—to a nuclear war is absurd. No one, president, Congress, or otherwise, should have that power.

At the moment, however, that power exists. And whatever the pros and cons, the precedents of Truman and Kennedy make clear that in today's reality it is the president, and not Congress, whose finger is on the nuclear button.

SHOULD THE MILITARY POWER
OF THE PRESIDENT
BE INCREASED—OR DECREASED?

Because of the vagueness of the Constitution, as interpreted over the years, the question of the war powers is really a question of relative power. Who is to have the greatest power, the president or Congress?

Those who favor presidential power argue that recent congressional measures have tied the hands of the president. Those who oppose presidential power argue that even more restraints are necessary. These arguments, still raging today, only echo those made at the Federal Convention over two hundred years ago.

Proponents of Congress and the presidency each argue that the institution they support is best qualified to make decisions of war and peace. Each can claim, with some historical justification, that their branch of government has been "right" at various times when the other branch has been "wrong." Certainly each has favored war in circumstances when the other has been inclined toward peace, and vice versa. Jefferson restrained Congress from war with England, but Polk pushed Congress toward war with Mexico. Congress pressed McKinley to take on the Spanish over Cuba, but Franklin Roosevelt maneuvered Congress into preparing for war with Germany. And so on.

Those who favor keeping—and even increasing—the presidential war powers argue that the United States faces a dangerous world. She has many enemies, and many interests that need to be protected. Sometimes, they argue, it is necessary to take military action short of war, either to fight those enemies or to protect those interests. And when those times come, it is necessary to act quickly and decisively. They argue, as some argued at the Federal Convention, that Congress is not equipped to do either. It is a deliberative body which finds it hard to act quickly; it is made up of two large bodies, each of which has to debate before it can act on important and controversial matters; and finally, when each branch of Congress has acted individually, the two must agree before approving an action. These realities almost inevitably make congressional action slow, and sometimes make it impossible.

And because Congress is a political institution—made up of hundreds of members, each of whom has his or her own constituency and own point of view—it finds it even harder to act decisively. The usual practice in Congress is compromise, and compromise is the enemy of decisive action. Compromise in planning and carrying out a military action can be fatal.

Walter Berns has argued flatly that "the Executive power is, in a sense, illimitable."[1] He claims that efforts to limit it, like the War Powers Resolution and the Oversight Act, are unwise. The chief executive must be free to act as circumstances dictate, he says, not according to rules laid down in advance by a legislative body. There is no way for Congress or anyone else to foresee all the possible circumstances a president may have to face. It is the nature of the presidency that the president has to have the power to act. If a president abuses that power, Berns and others point out, he or she can be impeached.

Besides, whatever members of Congress may say when complaining about presidential power, Congress has consistently shown its willingness to submit to presidential authority in practice. Even in the Mexican War, even in Vietnam—when congressional opposition was at its strongest—Congress never actually called a halt to hostilities over the wishes of the president.

Opponents of presidential power turn the same arguments around and use them against it. They agree that Congress has often been, in Raoul Berger's word, "supine." However, they say, that is hardly a reason for Congress to continue to surrender its authority to the president. Instead, it is a reason for Congress to reassert its own constitutional powers—the powers they say the framers intended it to have. In fact, Berger and others insist the surrender is, in itself, unconstitutional. A constitutional power cannot be delegated away, even if Congress wants to do so.

They agree with Sen. Daniel Patrick Moynihan that the world is "a dangerous place."[2] But, they argue, it is because of that fact—because of the enormous risks involved in *any* military action in a nuclear world—that such actions should only be taken after extended deliberation. They argue, along with James Wilson of Pennsylvania, a representative at the Constitutional Convention, that speed is not really a virtue when it comes to risking war. The main reason the Convention gave the power to declare war to Congress was, in Wilson's words, "to prevent the President from hurrying us into war."[3] They wanted to make sure that "no single man can involve us in such distress."[4] And if that was wise in those days of poor transportation and relatively primitive weapons, isn't it even more true today?

Seen in this light, the opponents argue, Congress' diversity—and its tendency to debate, to examine, and even to compromise—can be seen as a virtue and not a vice. It may sometimes be necessary to act decisively,

Right: *By arming Nicaraguan rebels, the U.S. managed to fight the Nicaraguan government without declaring war.* Below: *U.S. intervention often results in devastation for inhabitants of the invaded country—in this case, Vietnam.*

Top: *U.S. intervention also results in the loss of American property and lives. Thirty Americans were killed when an Iraqi missile hit the* U.S.S. Stark *in 1987.* Bottom: *U.S. soldiers carrying a wounded comrade in Vietnam, March 2, 1971. Although declared wars are just as destructive as undeclared wars, do you think that fulfilling the process of declaring war before committing troops might result in fewer wars and less destruction? Should presidents use their enormous power to launch undeclared wars or to avoid them?*

but only after all the consequences of military action have been thoroughly considered in advance.

Certainly, most opponents would admit, there may be the kind of unforeseen emergencies Berns talks about. There may even be exceptional cases (such as, possibly, the Civil War) in which a real and immediate danger to the survival of the nation actually justifies a president in stepping over his constitutional bounds. But these are special cases. They should not be used to justify the regular and constant undermining of the constitutional powers of Congress by the president.

There have been many conflicts between presidents and Congress over the war powers, but a 1969 Senate Foreign Relations Committee report claimed that what it saw as a systematic attempt to undermine congressional war power is actually quite new. "Only in the present century," it maintains, "have presidents used the Armed Forces of the United States against foreign governments entirely on their own authority, and only since 1950 [that is, since Truman ordered troops to Korea] have Presidents regarded themselves as having authority to commit the Armed Forces to full scale and sustained warfare."[5]

Still, as we have seen, presidents have been able to maneuver the country into war virtually from the beginning. It was the sixth president of the United States, John Quincy Adams, who wrote: "However startled we may be at the idea that the Executive Chief Magistrate has the power of involving the nation in war, without consulting Congress, an experience of fifty years has proved in numberless cases he has and must have exercised the power."[6]

There has not been a declared war since World War II, and yet America has fought two major wars (Korea and Vietnam) since that time, and been involved in many lesser conflicts as well. In recent years, Congress and the president have worked out various compromises (such as the Intelligence Oversight Act of 1980) which are supposedly designed to give Congress some role in such matters, while still allowing the president the flexibility almost everyone agrees may be needed in some circumstances. These compromises have consistently proven unsatisfactory in the eyes of many people in Congress. Presidents, they argue, have consistently treated such agreements with contempt. They have considered them, in the words of former Undersecretary of Defense Morton Halperin, only as "restrictions to get around by secrecy, trickery [and] illegal action."[7]

And yet such methods only work because Congress permits them to work. As Congressman Barney Frank has pointed out, Congress knows when it makes such compromises that they are not really compromises at all. They are, as Frank puts it, "transparent fig leaves" behind which presidents can do pretty much whatever they want to do.[8]

Nonetheless, presidents continually complain that Congress is interfering with their constitutional power to conduct foreign policy and to act as Commanders-in-Chief of the Army and Navy. In the 1970s, in the wake of Vietnam and the Watergate scandal, Congress briefly reasserted itself to the point where many critics began accusing Congress of "gutting" executive agencies like the CIA.

Pat M. Holt summed up the situation best in a report written for the American Enterprise Institute in 1978: "A short, nonlegal summary of the issue is that, at any given moment, the relative powers of the President and the Congress are what either feels it can get away with."[9] It was that way in the eighteenth century, when President Thomas Jefferson sent U.S. ships to battle the Barbary pirates before asking congressional permission to do so, and it is still that way today. It is likely to continue to be that way in the future.

NOTES

INTRODUCTION

1. For a journalistic account of the invasion of Grenada, see: *Time*, November 7, 1983, pp. 22–28. For more detailed information see: Hugh O'Shaughnessy's *Grenada: An Eyewitness Account of the U.S. Invasion and the Caribbean History That Provoked It* (New York: Dodd, Mead, 1985).
2. Ellen C. Collier, ed., *Instances of Use of United States Armed Forces Abroad, 1798–1983*, report issued by the Congressional Research Service, the Library of Congress, 1983.
3. *Background Information on the Use of U.S. Armed Forces in Foreign Countries, 1975 Revision*, prepared by the Foreign Affairs Division, Congressional Research Service, Library of Congress, printed for the use of the Committee on International Relations by the U.S. Government Printing Office, 1975, p. 28.

CHAPTER ONE

1. This famous remark, often misquoted as simply "War is hell," was made at a Grand Army of the Republic Convention in Columbus, Ohio, on August 11, 1880.
2. R. Ernest Dupuy and Trevor N. Dupuy, *The Encyclopedia of Military History from 3500 B.C. to the Present* (New York: Harper & Row, 1970), pp. 900–901.
3. Those interested in further information about pacifism should read *The Pacifist Conscience*, a collection of writings by pacif-

ists from Lao-Tzu to Martin Luther King, Jr., edited by Peter Mayer. (New York: Holt, Rinehart, and Winston, 1967).
4. For an academic discussion of some of these (and other) causes of war, see: *War: The Anthropology of Armed Conflict and Aggression*, edited by Morton Fried, Marvin Harris, and Robert Murphy (Garden City, N.Y.: The Natural History Press, 1968).
5. See: M. M. Bober, *Karl Marx's Interpretation of History*, 2nd edition (Cambridge, Mass.: Harvard University Press, 1948).
6. See: Karl von Clausewitz, *On War* (Princeton, N.J.: Princeton University Press, 1976).
7. The role of misunderstanding and miscalculation in starting wars is examined in Barbara Tuchman's *The March of Folly* (New York: Knopf, 1984). The same author's *The Guns of August* (New York: Macmillan, 1962) explores these factors in the events leading up to World War I.

CHAPTER TWO

1. For a detailed account of Shays' Rebellion, see M. L. Starkey's *A Little Rebellion* (New York: Knopf, 1955).
2. Although the proceedings of the Federal Convention were held in secret, some of the participants (including James Madison) kept notes of the debates. This book's discussion of the arguments made at the Convention is based largely on Max Farrand's collection of these notes, entitled *The Records of the Federal Convention of 1787*, paperback edition (New Haven and London: Yale University Press, 1966). Most of the quotes from Convention participants also come from it.
3. Farrand, vol. 2, p. 330.
4. Farrand, vol. 2, p. 329.
5. Farrand, vol. 2, p. 505.
6. Quoted by Raoul Berger in *Executive Privilege: A Constitutional Myth* (Cambridge: Harvard University Press, 1975), p. 61.
7. Both Butler quotes are from Farrand, vol. 2, p. 318.
8. Farrand, vol. 2, p. 318.
9. Farrand, vol. 2, p. 318.
10. Farrand, vol. 2, p. 318.
11. Farrand, vol. 2, p. 319.
12. Farrand, vol. 1, pp. 139–140.
13. Farrand, vol. 2, p. 319.
14. Farrand, vol. 2, p. 548
15. Quoted by Charles Warren in *The Making of the Constitution* (New York: Little, Brown, 1929), in a footnote, p. 481.

CHAPTER THREE

1. Reginald Horsman, *The War of 1812* (New York: Knopf, 1969), page 55. For a book-length account of the war, see it, or J.C.A. Staggs', *Mr. Madison's War* (Princeton, N.J.: Princeton University Press, 1983).
2. Richard N. Current, T. Harry Williams, and Frank Freidel, *American History: A Survey*, 4th edition (New York: Knopf, 1975), p. 188.
3. Current et al., pp. 210–211.
4. Horsman, pp. 24.
5. See Staggs'; *Mr. Madison's War* for a discussion of this.
6. Quoted by Berger, p. 79.
7. Arthur Bernon Tourtellot, *The Presidents on the Presidency* (Garden City, N.Y.: Doubleday, 1964), p. 318.
8. Current et al., p. 345.
9. Robert Leckie, *The Wars of America* (New York: Harper & Row, 1968), p. 326.
10. Frederick Merk, *Dissent in Three American Wars* (Cambridge: Harvard University Press, 1970), p. 35. This book is made up of three essays, one by Merk and the others by Samuel Eliot Morison and Frank Freidel.
11. Merk, *Dissent*, p. 35.
12. Leckie, p. 326.
13. Current et al., p. 350.
14. Leckie, p. 327.
15. Merk, *Dissent*, p. 35.
16. Quoted by Merk, *Dissent*, p. 50.
17. Leckie, p. 327.
18. Quoted by Arthur M. Schlesinger, Jr., in Rexford G. Tugwell and Thomas E. Cronin, eds., *The Presidency Reappraised: Congress and the Making of American Foreign Policy* (New York: Praeger, 1974), p. 87.
19. Quoted by Tourtellot, p. 310.
20. Quoted by Tourtellot, p. 323.
21. Adolf A. Berle in *The Presidency Reappraised*, p. 75.
22. Leckie, p. 545.
23. Leckie, p. 547.
24. George Fort Milton, *The Use of Presidential Power 1789–1943* (New York: Little, Brown, 1944), p. 51.
25. Leckie, p. 546.
26. Current et al., p. 549.
27. Schlesinger, *The Imperial Presidency*, p. 82.
28. Quoted in Samuel Eliot Morison's *The Oxford History of the*

American People (New York: Oxford University Press, 1965), p. 848.

29. Current et al., p. 613.
30. Berger, p. 83.
31. Current et al., p. 615.
32. Allan Nevins and Henry Steele Commager, *A Pocket History of the United States,* 7th edition (New York: Washington Square Press, 1981), p. 396.
33. Current et al., pp. 616–617.
34. Collier, pp. 13–14.
35. Leckie, p. 708.
36. Leckie, p. 709.
37. Quoted by Morison, *History,* p. 995.
38. Quoted by Leckie, p. 711.
39. Quoted by Morison, *History,* pp. 998–999.
40. Current et al., p. 701.
41. Collier, p. 14.
42. Morison, *History* p. 999.
43. Current et al., p. 707.
44. For a brief discussion of this controversy, see "The Background of Pearl Harbor," in *American History,* p. 705; for a longer review, see *Pearl Harbor: Warning and Decision,* by Roberta Wohlstetter (Palo Alto, Calif.: Stanford University Press, 1962).
45. Clinton Rossiter, "The Presidency—Focus of Leadership", *New York Times Magazine,* November 11, 1956, reprinted in *The American President* (Englewood Cliffs, N.J.: Prentice-Hall, 1967), p. 80.

CHAPTER FOUR

1. Milton, p. 110.
2. Tourtellot, p. 332.
3. Tourtellot, p. 331.
4. Quoted by Milton, p. 111.
5. Tourtellot, p. 332.
6. Marcus Raskin, Fund for New Priorities symposium, "Is Executive Power Undermining Our Constitution?", held in Washington, D.C., March 18, 1987, and carried live over the C-SPAN Television Network.
7. Leon Friedman and Burt Neuborne, *Unquestioning Obedience to the President: The ACLU Case Against the Illegal War in Vietnam* (New York: Norton, 1972), pp. 126, 205–206.
8. Milton, p. 110.

9. Friedman and Neuborne, p. 206.
10. Quoted by Berger, p. 80.
11. Milton, p. 118.
12. For a discussion of *ex parte Milligan*, see Darwin Kelley's *Milligan's Fight Against Lincoln* (Pompano Beach, Fla.: Exposition, 1973).
13. Current et al., pp. 386–387.
14. Thomas H. Johnson, in consultation with Harvey Wish, *The Oxford Companion to American History* (New York: Oxford University Press, 1966), p. 272.
15. Milton, p. 119.
16. Milton, p. 119.
17. Johnson, p. 32.
18. Quoted by Milton, p. 120.
19. R. Gordon Hoxie, *Command Decision and the Presidency* (New York: Reader's Digest Press, 1977), p. 42.
20. Nevins and Commager, p. 225.
21. Milton, p. 121.

CHAPTER FIVE
1. Berger, p. 86.
2. Edward S. Corwin, *Total War and the Constitution* (New York: Knopf, 1947), p. 146.
3. Arthur M. Schlesinger, Jr. and Alfred de Grazia, *Congress and the Presidency*, Rational Debate Seminar (Washington, D.C.: American Enterprise Institute, 1967), p. 22.
4. Julius W. Pratt, *A History of United States Foreign Policy,* 3rd edition (Englewood Cliffs, N.J.: Prentice-Hall, 1972), pp. 58–59.
5. Collier, p. 2.
6. Quoted by Schlesinger in *The Presidency Reappraised*, p. 84.
7. See Berger, p. 75.
8. These and the other examples which follow are taken from Collier's *Instances of Use.*
9. Pratt, p. 141.
10. Collier, p. 5.
11. Pratt, p. 142.
12. Quoted by Leckie, p. 566.
13. Leckie, p. 574.
14. Current et al., p. 605.
15. Hoxie, p. 41.
16. Quoted by Nevins and Commager, pp. 371–372.
17. Arthur M. Schlesinger, Jr. *The Imperial Presidency* (Boston: Houghton Mifflin, 1973), p. 55.

18. Current et al., p. 607.
19. Friedman and Neuborne, p. 137.
20. Current et al., p. 608.
21. Morison, *Oxford History*, p. 845.
22. Morison, *Oxford History* p. 846.
23. See Collier.
24. See "Why Are the Marines in Lebanon?," *Newsweek,* November 7, 1983, pp. 93–94.
25. "All Hell Breaking Loose," *Time*, February 20, 1984, pp. 34–35.
26. *The Americana Annual 1985* (Danbury, Conn.: Grolier, 1985), p. 552.
27. For an interesting, if controversial, account of the Libyan raid, see "Target Qaddafi," by Seymour Hersh, *New York Times Magazine*, February 22, 1987.
28. Collier, p. 12.
29. Quoted by Bert Cochran in *Harry Truman and the Crisis Presidency* (New York: Funk and Wagnalls, 1973), p. 173.
30. Hoxie, p. 90.
31. Hoxie pp. 90–91.
32. Hoxie, p. 9.
33. Richard L. Tobin, *Decisions of Destiny* (Cleveland: World, 1961), p. 261.
34. Quoted by Tobin, pp. 262–263.
35. Quoted by Tobin, p. 260.

CHAPTER SIX

1. For the basic chronology of the American involvement in Vietnam, I have relied on "Chronology: Generation of Conflict," *Time,* November 6, 1972, pp. 28–29.
2. Current et al., p. 816.
3. *Time*, November 6, 1972, p. 28.
4. Current et al., p. 817.
5. This account of the events in the Gulf of Tonkin and President Johnson's response relies largely on two contemporary newsmagazine reports: "A Measured and Fitting Response," *Time,* August 14, 1964, and "Vietnam: 'We Seek No Wider War,' " *Newsweek,* August 17, 1964.
6. *Newsweek,* August 17, 1964, p. 17.
7. *Time*, August 14, 1964, p. 15.
8. Friedman and Neuborne, p. 147.
9. *Time*, August 14, 1964, p. 16.
10. Friedman and Neuborne, p. 193.
11. *Newsweek,* August 17, 1964, p. 18.

12. Berger, p. 85.
13. Quoted in Friedman and Neuborne, p. 144.
14. Friedman and Neuborne, p. 148.
15. This summary of objections to the American involvement is based on the arguments made by Senator George S. McGovern in his Introduction to *Unquestioning Obedience*, 9–20.
16. Current et al., p. 817.
17. *Time* "Chronology," p. 29.
18. McGovern, p. 14.
19. Quoted by Berger, p. 87.
20. Defense Department figures, quoted by McGovern, p. 12.
21. James R. Dickenson, "New Moves to Curb War Powers," *The National Observer*, July 28, 1973, p. 2.
22. Quoted by McGovern, p. 15.
23. Quoted by McGovern, p. 16.
24. Quoted by Nevins and Commager, p. 568.

CHAPTER SEVEN

1. Quoted by Louis Fisher, *The Presidency Reappraised*, pp. 57–58.
2. Friedman and Neuborne, p. 26.
3. Quoted in Friedman and Neuborne, p. 26.
4. Quoted in Friedman and Neuborne, p. 250.
5. Friedman and Neuborne, p. 273.
6. Public Law 93–148 (the War Powers Resolution) is available from the U.S. Government Printing Office, Washington, D.C.
7. Richard L. Lyons, "Congress Overrides Veto, Enacts War Curb," *Washington Post*, November 8, 1973, p. 1.
8. *Time*, November 7, 1983, p. 50.
9. Pat M. Holt, *The War Powers Resolution: The Role of Congress in United States Armed Intervention* (Washington, D.C.: American Enterprise Institute, 1978), p. 1.
10. Ellen Collier, "The War Powers Resolution: A Decade of Experience." Report #84-22 F, Congressional Research Service of the Library of Congress, p. 26.
11. Collier, "The War Powers Resolution," p. 16.
12. Collier, "The War Powers Resolution," p. 8.
13. Quoted by Collier, "The War Powers Resolution," p. 35.
14. Quoted by Collier, "The War Powers Resolution," p. 21.
15. "U.S. Says Copters, Answering Shots, Sank 3 Iran Boats," *New York Times*, October 9, 1987, p. 1.
16. Reported by CBS News, October 12, 1987.
17. Reported on "The MacNeil/Lehrer Report," the Public Broadcasting Service, October 21, 1987.

18. News conference, broadcast live over the C-SPAN television network, October 21, 1987.
19. Walter Berns, Fund for New Priorities Symposium: "Is Executive Power Undermining Our Constitution?;" March 18, 1987. Order from: Fund for New Priorities in America, 24 E. 35 St., New York, NY 10016.
20. Congressman Barney Frank, Fund for New Priorities Symposium.
21. This is how former Undersecretary of Defense Morton Halperin referred to the Reagan administration's interpretation of "timely" in testimony before a House committee on April 8, 1987.
22. *Time*, August 17, 1987, p. 21.

CHAPTER EIGHT

1. Tobin, pp. 248–249.
2. Theodore C. Sorensen, *Kennedy* (New York: Harper & Row, 1965), p. 704.
3. Sorensen, p. 702.

CHAPTER NINE

1. Berns, Fund for New Priorities Symposium.
2. This phrase is, in fact, the title of an interesting book by Moynihan, written out of his experience as United States Ambassador to the United Nations.
3. Quoted by Berger, Fund for New Priorities Symposium.
4. Quoted by Berger, *Executive Privilege*, p. 61.
5. National Commitments Report of the Senate Foreign Relations Committee, April 16, 1969, p. 31.
6. Quoted by Schlesinger, p. 22.
7. Morton Halperin, Fund for New Priorities Symposium.
8. Frank, Fund for New Priorities Symposium.
9. Holt, p. 1.

FOR FURTHER READING

The following government reports, listing American military involvement in military conflicts abroad, are available from the Government Printing Office:

Collier, Ellen C., ed., *Instances of Use of United States Armed Forces Abroad, 1798–1983*, issued by the Congressional Research Service, The Library of Congress, 1983.

Background Information on the Use of U.S. Armed Forces in Foreign Countries, 1975 Revision, prepared by the Foreign Affairs Division, Congressional Research Service, Library of Congress.

For historical background on some of the most significant conflicts and policies referred to in this book:

Cochran, Bert. *Harry Truman and the Crisis Presidency.* New York: Funk and Wagnalls, 1973.

Horsman, Reginald. *The War of 1812.* New York: Knopf, 1969.

O'Shaughnessy, Hugh. *Grenada: An Eyewitness Account of the U.S. Invasion and the Caribbean History That Provoked It.* New York: Dodd, Mead, 1985.

Pratt, Julius W. *A History of United States Foreign Policy.* Englewood Cliffs, N.J.: Prentice-Hall, 1972.

Starkey, M. L. *A Little Rebellion.* New York: Knopf, 1955.

Staggs, J.C.A. *Mr. Madison's War.* Princeton, N.J.: Princeton University Press, 1983.

Tobin, Richard L. *Decisions of Destiny.* Cleveland: World, 1961.

For discussions of some of the issues raised in this book:

Berger, Raoul. *Executive Privilege: A Constitutional Myth.* Cambridge, Mass.: Harvard University Press, 1975.

Corwin, Edward S. *Total War and the Constitution.* New York: Knopf, 1947.

Eagleton, Thomas F. *War and Presidential Power: A Chronology of Congressional Surrender.* New York: Liveright, 1974.

Friedman, Leon, and Neuborne, Burt. *Unquestioning Obedience to the President: The ACLU Case Against the Illegal War in Vietnam.* New York: Norton, 1972.

Hoxie, R. Gordon. *Command Decision and the Presidency.* New York: Reader's Digest Press, 1977.

Javits, Jacob P., with Kellerman, Don. *Who Makes War: The President versus the Congress.* New York: Morrow, 1973.

Milton, George Fort. *The Use of Presidential Power 1789–1943.* New York: Little, Brown, 1944.

Schlesinger, Arthur M., Jr. *The Imperial Presidency.* Boston: Houghton Mifflin, 1973.

Schlesinger, Arthur M., Jr., and de Grazia, Alfred. *Congress and the Presidency*, Rational Debate Seminar, Washington, D.C.: American Enterprise Institute, 1967.

Tugwell, Rexford G., and Cronin, Thomas E., eds. *The Presidency Reappraised: Congress and the Making of American Foreign Policy.* New York: Praeger, 1974.

Two interesting but very different books that shed light on how the decisions that lead to war are made:

Fried, Morton; Harris, Marvin; and Murphy, Robert, eds. *War: The Anthropology of Armed Conflict and Aggression.* Garden City, N.Y.: The Natural History Press. 1968.

Tuchman, Barbara. *The March of Folly.* New York: Knopf, 1984.

On the War Powers Act:

Collier, Ellen. "The War Powers Resolution: A Decade of Experience." Report #84-22 F, Congressional Research Service of the Library of Congress.

Holt, Pat M. *The War Powers Resolution: The Role of Congress in United States Armed Intervention.* Washington, D.C.: American Enterprise Institute, 1978.

INDEX

New York *World*, 52, 66
Ngo Dinh Diem, 89, 90
Nicaragua, 74, 75, 79–80, 111,
    116, 117, *126*
Nixon, Richard M., 94–95, 98,
    99, *100,* 101, 103, 107
Nuclear warfare, 14, 84, 118–
    22

O'Sullivan, John L., 46

Pacifists, 15
Pakistan, 89
Palestine, 75
Panama, 75
Panama Canal, 77–78
Peace treaties, 28, 36–38
Pearl Harbor, 17, 60–61, *60*
Perry, Matthew, 76, 79
Pershing, John J., 81
Persian Gulf, 11, 112–14, *113,*
    115
Philippines, 53, 76–77, 89
Pierce, Franklin, 79
Pinckney, Charles, 29
Polk, James K., 46–51, *49,* 123
Porter, David, 79
Posses comitatus, 62
President, U.S.:
    checking power of, 102–17
    as Commander-in-Chief,
        35–36, 38, 50–51, 56,
        69–70
    impeachment of, 102, 103
    nuclear weapons and,
        118–22
    peace power of, 37–38
    war powers of, 10–11, 22,
        28, 30–34, 35–36, 38,
        43–45, 62–66, 86, 94,
        95–96, 123–29
    see also specific presi-
        dents
Prize cases, 65–66

Protestant Reformation, 19–20
Puerto Rico, 53, 77, 79
Pulitzer, Joseph, 51–52

Racism, 20
Raskin, Marcus, 64
Reagan, Ronald, 10, 11, 75,
    81–83, 109–14, *109, 113,*
    115, *116,* 117
Religious conflicts, 19–20
Retaliation, 79–83
Revolutionary wars, 12, 17, 77–
    78, 80–81, 84
    American, 11, 17, 18, 23,
        24, 27, 39
Roosevelt, Franklin D., 54, 57–
    61, *58, 60,* 72, 123
Roosevelt, Theodore, 52, 53,
    57, 77–78, *78*
Russian Revolution, 84

Schlesinger, Arthur M., Jr., 53
Self-defense, 17
Senate, U.S., 36–38, 49, 94,
    97, 99–101, 117, 128
    see also Congress, U.S.
Shays' Rebellion, 24–26, *25*
Sherman, William Tecumseh,
    12–14, *13*
Slavery, 50, 66–70
Sorensen, Theodore, 121
Southeast Aisa Treaty Organi-
    zation (SEATO), 89, 94
Soviet Union, 21, 84, 88, 119,
    120, *120*
Spain, 27, 39, 41, 77
Spanish-American War, 51–53,
    52, 76, *78,* 123
Stark, 127, 112
States:
    power of federal govern-
        ment vs., 23–24, 25–26,
        27–28, 67
    taxation by, 24–25